Philippine Freycinetia: The Oaks Of The Philippines

Elmer Drew Merrill

In the interest of creating a more extensive selection of rare historical book reprints, we have chosen to reproduce this title even though it may possibly have occasional imperfections such as missing and blurred pages, missing text, poor pictures, markings, dark backgrounds and other reproduction issues beyond our control. Because this work is culturally important, we have made it available as a part of our commitment to protecting, preserving and promoting the world's literature. Thank you for your understanding.

PHILIPPINE FREYCINETIA

THE OAKS OF THE PHILIPPINES

THE GENUS RADERMACHERA HASSK.,
IN THE PHILIPPINES

By Elmer D. Merrill

(From the Botanical Section of the Biological Laboratory, Bureau of Science, Manila, P. I.)

Reprinted from
THE PHILIPPINE JOURNAL OF SCIENCE
Published by the Bureau of Science of the Philippine Government, Manila, P. I.
Vol. III, No. 5, Section C, Botany, October, 1908

MANILA
BUREAU OF PRINTING
1908

31820
Feb. 17, 1919

PREVIOUS PUBLICATIONS OF THE BUREAU OF GOVERNMENT LABORATORIES.

[1] No. 1, 1902, Biological Laboratory.—Preliminary Report of the Appearance in the Philippine Islands of a Disease Clinically Resembling Glanders. By R. P. Strong, M. D.

No. 2, 1902, Chemical Laboratory.—The Preparation of Benzoyl-Acetyl Peroxide and its Use as an Intestinal Antiseptic in Cholera and Dysentery. Preliminary Notes. By Paul C. Freer, M. D., Ph. D.

[1] No. 3, 1903, Biological Laboratory.—A Preliminary Report on Trypanosomiasis of Horses in the Philippine Islands. By W. E. Musgrave, M. D., and Norman E. Williamson.

[1] No. 4, 1903, Serum Laboratory.—Preliminary Report on the Study of Rinderpest of Cattle and Carabaos in the Philippine Islands. By James W. Jobling, M. D.

[1] No. 5, 1903, Biological Laboratory.—Trypanosoma and Trypanosomiasis, with Special Reference to Surra in the Philippine Islands. By W. E. Musgrave, M. D., and Moses T. Clegg.

[1] No. 6, 1903.—New and Noteworthy Plants, I. The American Element in the Philippine Flora. By Elmer D. Merrill, Botanist. (Issued January 20, 1904.)

[1] No. 7, 1903, Chemical Laboratory.—The Gutta Percha and Rubber of the Philippine Islands. By Penoyer L. Sherman, jr., Ph. D.

[1] No. 8, 1903.—A Dictionary of the Plant Names of the Philippine Islands. By Elmer D. Merrill, Botanist.

[1] No. 9, 1903, Biological and Serum Laboratories.—A Report on Hæmorrhagic Septicæmia in Animals in the Philippine Islands. By Paul G. Woolley, M. D., and J. W. Jobling, M. D.

[1] No. 10, 1903, Biological Laboratory.—Two Cases of a Peculiar Form of Hand Infection (Due to an Organism Resembling the Koch-Weeks Bacillus). By John R. McDill, M. D., and Wm. B. Wherry, M. D.

[1] No. 11, 1903, Biological Laboratory.—Entomological Division, Bulletin No. 1: Preliminary Bulletin on Insects of the Cacao. (Prepared Especially for the Benefit of Farmers.) By Charles S. Banks, Entomologist.

[1] No. 12, 1903, Biological Laboratory.—Report on Some Pulmonary Lesions Produced by the Bacillus of Hæmorrhagic Septicæmia of Carabaos. By Paul G. Woolley, M. D.

No. 13, 1904, Biological Laboratory.—A Fatal Infection by a Hitherto Undescribed Chromogenic Bacterium: Bacillus Aureus Fœtidus. By Maximilian Herzog, M. D.

[1] No. 14, 1904.—Serum Laboratory: Texas Fever in the Philippine Islands and the Far East. By J. W. Jobling, M. D., and Paul G. Woolley, M. D. Biological Laboratory: Entomological Division, Bulletin No. 2: The Australian Tick (Boophilus Australis Fuller) in the Philippine Islands. By Charles S. Banks, Entomologist.

No. 15, 1904, Biological and Serum Laboratories.—Report on Bacillus Violaceus Manilæ: A Pathogenic Micro-Organism. By Paul G. Woolley, M. D.

[1] No. 16, 1904, Biological Laboratory.—Protective Inoculation Against Asiatic Cholera: An Experimental Study. By Richard P. Strong, M. D.

No. 17, 1904.—New or Noteworthy Philippine Plants, II. By Elmer D. Merrill, Botanist.

[1] No. 18, 1904, Biological Laboratory.—I. Amebas: Their Cultivation and Etiologic Significance. By W. E. Musgrave, M. D., and Moses T. Clegg. II. The Treatment of Intestinal Amœbiasis (Amœbic Dysentery) in the Tropics. By W. E. Musgrave, M. D.

No. 19, 1904, Biological Laboratory.—Some Observations on the Biology of the Cholera Spirillum. By W. B. Wherry, M. D.

No. 20, 1904.—Biological Laboratory: I. Does Latent or Dormant Plague Exist Where the Disease is Endemic? By Maximilian Herzog, M. D., and Charles B. Hare. Serum Laboratory: II. Broncho-Pneumonia of Cattle; Its Association with B. Bovisepticus. By Paul G. Woolley, M. D., and Walter Sorrell, D. V. S. III. Pinto (Paño Blanco). By Paul G. Woolley, M. D. Chemical Laboratory: IV. Notes on Analysis of the Water from the Manila Water Supply. By Charles L. Bliss, M. S. Serum Laboratory: V. Frambœsia: Its Occurrence in Natives in the Philippine Islands. By Paul G. Woolley, M. D.

No. 21, 1904, Biological Laboratory.—Some Questions Relating to the Virulence of Micro-Organisms with Particular Reference to Their Immunizing Powers. By Richard P. Strong, M. D.

No. 22, 1904, Bureau of Government Laboratories.—I. A Description of the New Buildings of the Bureau of Government Laboratories. By Paul C. Freer, M. D., Ph. D. II. A Catalogue of the Library of the Bureau of Government Laboratories. By Mary Polk, Librarian.

[1] No. 23, 1904, Biological Laboratory.—Plague: Bacteriology, Morbid Anatomy, and Histopathology (Including a Consideration of Insects as Plague Carriers). By Maximilian Herzog, M. D.

No. 24, 1904, Biological Laboratory.—Glanders: Its Diagnosis and Prevention (Together with a Report on Two Cases of Human Glanders Occurring in Manila and Some Notes on the Bacteriology and Polymorphism of Bacterium Mallei). By William B. Wherry, M. D.

No. 25, 1904.[2]—Birds from the Islands of Romblon, Sibuyan, and Cresta de Gallo. By Richard C. McGregor.

No. 26, 1904, Biological Laboratory.—The Clinical and Pathological Significance of Balantidium Coli. By Richard P. Strong, M. D.

No. 27, 1904.—A Review of the Identification of the Species Described in Blanco's Flora de Filipinas. By Elmer D. Merrill, Botanist.

No. 28, 1904.—I. The Polypodiaceæ of the Philippine Islands. II. Edible Philippine Fungi. By Edwin B. Copeland, Ph. D.

No. 29, 1904.—I. New or Noteworthy Philippine Plants, III. II. The Source of Manila Elemi. By Elmer D. Merrill, Botanist.

No. 30, 1905, Chemical Laboratory.—I. Autocalytic Decomposition of Silver Oxide. II. Hydration in Solution. By Gilbert N. Lewis, Ph. D.

No. 31, 1905, Biological Laboratory.—I. Notes on a Case of Hæmatochyluria (Together with Some Observations on the Morphology of the Embryo Nematode, Filaria Nocturna). By William B. Wherry, M. D., and John R. McDill, M. D., Manila, P. I. II. A Search Into the Nitrate and Nitrite Content of Witte's "Peptone," with Special Reference to Its Influence on the Demonstration of the Indol and Cholera-Red Reactions. By William B. Wherry, M. D.

---

[1] Out of print.

[2] The first four bulletins in the ornithological series were published by the Ethnological Survey under the title "Bulletins of the Philippine Museum." Later ornithological publications of the Government appeared as publications of the Bureau of Government Laboratories.

(Concluded on third page of cover.)

PHILIPPINE FREYCINETIA.

By Elmer D. Merrill.

(From the Botanical Section of the Biological Laboratory, Bureau of Science, Manila, P. I.)

Philippine *Pandanaceae* had received little attention before the year 1900 either from collectors or systematists. However, in 1900, Warburg published his monograph of the family,[1] recognizing three genera, *Sararanga*, a monotypic genus, its single species, *S. sinuosa* Hemsl., known only from the Solomon Islands and New Guinea, *Freycinetia* with 62 species, extending from Ceylon and Burma to Formosa, Malaya, northern Australia, Polynesia, and the Hawaiian Islands, with 7 species in the Philippines, and *Pandanus* with 156 species, extending from tropical Africa to tropical Asia, Malaya, Australia, and Polynesia, with but a single species definitely recorded from the Philippines, and five Philippine species described by Blanco considered as doubtful ones.

Before the publication of Warburg's monograph four species of *Freycinetia* had been described from the Philippines by various authors, Warburg adding three additional ones, but recent collections have added a considerable number of species of the genus to the known Philippine flora, while a second species of *Sararanga*, (*S. philippinensis* Merr.), has been found on the east coasts of Luzon and Samar, and a large number of species of *Pandanus* have been described and the status determined of most of Blanco's imperfectly described species.

In Martelli's recent paper on the Philippine species of *Pandanus*[2] twenty-three species with several varieties are recognized as occurring in the Archipelago, beside three doubtful species, while more recent collections have added two or three additional ones to the list. As many of the species of *Pandanus* and *Freycinetia* are very local, it is very probable that we do not know more than one-half the species of either genus actually growing in the Philippines.

The first species of *Freycinetia* described from the Philippines was *F. luzonensis* Presl Epim. Bot. (1851) 238, but previously Gaudichaud had figured, but not described, what is apparently the same species

[1] Pflanzenreich **3** (1900) 1–97.
[2] *This Journal* **3** (1908) *Bot.* 59–72.

under the name of *F. cumingiana,* and also a second Philippine species, *F. sphaerocephala,* in the Botany of the Voyage of the Bonite, Atlas, 1843. In 1883, Naves in the Novissima Appendix to the third edition of Blanco's Flora de Filipinas, 285, 286, enumerates four species, which are all, with the possible exception of *F. luzonensis,* admitted on erroneous identifications, and can be ignored. He reduced *Tillandsia pseudo-ananas* Blanco to *Freycinetia insignis* Blume, but this is a manifest error, as an examination of Blanco's description shows conclusively that *Tillandsia pseudo-ananas* can not be a *Freycinetia,* but is probably a *Pandanus,* and possibly the same as *P. copelandii* Merr. Blanco did not consider any species of *Freycinetia* in his Flora de Filipinas.

Having recently had an opportunity to examine the types or authentic material of all the Philippine species considered by Warburg, in the herbaria at Kew and Berlin, it became evident that a certain number of recently described forms were invalid, three of the species described by Mr. Elmer, and one by myself. In justice to Mr. Elmer, however, it is manifest that the determination of two of his species as new, *F. lucbanensis* and *F. confusa,* was due to errors in Warburg's monograph, the former being identical with *F. ferox* Warb., the leaves of the type of which are about 1 m long but described as 30 cm long, the latter being the same as *F. vidalii* Hemsl. The affinity of the latter was recognized by Mr. Elmer, but Hemsley's species was placed by Warburg in the wrong section of the genus, the type being a very immature specimen.

In view of the fact that a recent paper has been published on Philippine *Pandanus,* it has been thought advisable to prepare a list of the known species of the other large genus in the family, *Freycinetia,* giving also a provisional key to the species. Twenty-four species are recognized, all of which are endemic in the Philippines, so far as is known, giving the Archipelago a far greater known number of species than any other geographical region in which the genus is found. Luzon alone has eighteen species, while the region about Mount Banajao, Province of Tayabas, Luzon, is remarkable in having no less than eleven species of the genus, more than are known from any single island in the Malayan region; New Guinea and the Malay Peninsula coming first with but eight species, Celebes next with seven, Java with six, Borneo and New Caledonia with four each, Sumatra with three, and various other islands with one or two species each. The above distribution list is based largely on Warburg's monograph, and the number of species actually known from some of the above islands may be larger than the figures given, while undoubtedly a great many undescribed forms remain to be collected.

Stigmas 1 to 3, usually 2. § OLIGOSTIGMA.
  Leaves about 1 m long, 5 to 8 cm wide.
    Leaves long and gradually acuminate; syncarps 3-nate, about 3 cm in diameter.
        1. *F. ferox*
    Leaves abruptly acuminate; syncarps 3- or 4-nate, 5 to 7 cm in diameter.
        2. *F. maxima*
  Leaves much less than 1 m long.
    Leaves oblong, 3.5 to 4.5 cm wide, abruptly short-acuminate.. 3. *F. oblongifolia*
    Leaves lanceolate or linear-lanceolate, 2.5 cm wide or less, usually slenderly long-acuminate.
      Leaves 10 to 15 cm, rarely 18 cm long................................ 4. *F. luzonensis*
      Leaves 20 to 60 cm long.
        Syncarps 2 cm long or less; leaves about 40 cm long, 5 to 6 mm wide.
          5. *F. vidalii*
        Syncarps 4 to 11 cm long.
          Mature syncarps about 4 cm long.
            Leaves about 20 cm long.. 6. *F. robinsonii*
            Leaves 40 to 50 cm long.. 7. *F. curranii*
          Mature syncarps 7 to 11 cm long.
            Syncarps 4–6-nate, about 7 cm long; leaves 20 to 30 cm long.
              8. *F. multiflora*
            Syncarps ternate, about 11 cm long; leaves 40 to 60 cm long.
              9. *F. auriculata*
Stigmas 3 to 10. § PLEIOSTIGMA.
  Syncarps cylindrical, 3 to 5 times as long as broad.
    Leaves 2 cm wide or less.
      Leaves 20 to 25 cm long, gradually narrowed upwards to the long and slenderly acuminate apex; syncarps binate or ternate, 2.5 to 3.5 cm long .... 10. *F. palawanensis*
      Leaves 10 to 18 cm long, not caudate-acuminate; syncarps 4-nate or 5-nate, 2 cm long or less... 11. *F. jagorii*
    Leaves 2.5 to 5.5 cm wide.
      Leaves abruptly short-acuminate.
        Leaves 30 to 40 cm long, margins scabrous near the base and apex only, the median portions smooth.................................... 12. *F. philippinensis*
        Leaves about 1 m long, margins scabrous throughout............ 13. *F. rigida*
      Leaves gradually and slenderly long-acuminate.
        Leaf margins scabrous only near the base and apex............ 14. *F. scabripes*
        Leaf margins scabrous throughout.
          Leaf base dilated, the stipule free above............................ 15. *F. dilatata*
          Leaf base not dilated, the stipule attached along one side throughout its length .... 16. *F. negrosensis*
  Syncarps globose or subglobose.
    Leaves 4 to 5 cm wide, abruptly short-acuminate.
      Leaves strongly auricled at the base.. 17. *F. merrillii*
      Leaves not auricled at the base.. 18. *F. megacarpa*
    Leaves not exceeding 2 cm in width.
      Leaves 2 to 3 mm wide.. 19. *F. monocephala*
      Leaves 7 to 20 mm wide.
        Leaves 6 cm long or less... 20. *F. sphaerocephala*
        Leaves exceeding 6 cm in length.
          Leaves 1.5 to 2 cm wide.
            Leaves 9 to 13 cm long... 21. *F. rostrata*
            Leaves about 20 cm long.. 22. *F. warburgii*
          Leaves less than 1 cm wide.
            Leaves less than 10 cm long....................................... 23. *F. ensifolia*
            Leaves 15 to 25 cm long... 24. *F. williamsii*

1. **Freycinetia ferox** Warb. Pflanzenreich 3 (1900) 33.
Freycinetia lucbanensis Elm. Leafl. Philip. Bot. 1 (1907) 212.

LUZON, without locality, *Warburg s. n.*, in Herb. Berol. (type), carbon impression in Herb. Bur. Sci.: Province of Tayabas, Lucban, *Elmer 8230*, May, 1907, type of *Freycinetia lucbanensis* Elm.

The species described by Elmer is identical with that of Warburg, but neither specimen is mature. In the original description of the species Warburg erroneously describes the leaf as 30 cm long, but the type, which I have examined in Herb. Berol., has leaves about 1 m long, Warburg's "30 cm" being a typographical error for, probably, 80 cm. Because of this error, Mr. Elmer did not recognize the identity of his plant with Warburg's species. The type of *F. ferox* Warb. was from central Luzon, probably Tayabas Province.

2. **Freycinetia maxima** sp. nov. § *Oligostigma*.

Robusta, scandens, ramis circiter 3 cm diametro, teretibus; foliis numerosis, dense imbricatis, flaccide-coriaceis, utrinque reticulatis, 0.5 ad 1 m longis, 7 ad 8 cm latis, anguste oblongo-lanceolatis vel lanceolatis, apice abrupte breviter acuminatis, basi paullo augustatis ibique marginibus membranaceis pallidis vel purpureis 6 ad 15 cm longis, usque ad 2 cm latis, instructis, totis marginibus valde spinuloso-serratis, costa subtus, in partibus superioribus, spinulosis. Spadicibus fructiferis ternis vel quaternis, oblongo-ellipsoideis vel anguste oblongo-obovoideis, 15 cm longis, 6 ad 7 cm diametro, leviter longitudinaliter sulcatis vel subcylindraceis; pedunculis circiter 2.5 cm longis, 1 cm crassis; fructibus immaturis linearibus, 1.5 cm longis, 1 mm diametro; stigmatibus 2 vel 3.

LUZON, Province of Tayabas, Malicboi, *For. Bur. 10754 Curran*, July 22, 1908; Albay-Sorsogon, Adumoy Hills, *For. Bur. 12381 Curran*, June, 1908.

A species apparently most closely allied to the preceding and to *Freycinetia latispina* Warb., of Celebes, but distinct from both, and from all other described forms. It is remarkable for its large leaves, which are relatively broad, strongly reticulate, on their margins and in the upper part of the lower surface of the midrib, strongly spinescent, but more especially remarkable for its very large syncarps, each composed of several thousand fruits.

3. **Freycinetia oblongifolia** sp. nov. § *Oligostigma*.

Robusta, scandens, circiter 4 m alta; ramis teretibus, 1 cm crassis; foliis submembranaceis, oblongis vel oblongo-lanceolatis, circiter 20 cm longis, 4 ad 5 cm latis, basi angustatis, haud vaginantibus; apice breviter abrupteque acuminatis, margine prope basin apicemque denticulatis, in media parte inermibus. Inflorescentiis terminalibus, spadicibus femineis ternis vel quaternis, bracteis multis imbricatis roseis, acutis vel acuminatis, marginibus costisque glabris vel apicem versus dentatis, exterioribus 1 ad 2 cm longis, circiter 1.5 cm latis, interioribus 6 ad 8 cm longis, 2.5 ad 3 cm latis, circumdatis. Spadicibus fructiferis, cylindraceis, aurantiacis, circiter 7 cm longis, 2 cm latis; fructibus circiter 2.5 mm diametro basi plus minus succulentis, supra lignosis, angulatis; stigmatibus 2.

MINDANAO, Province of Surigao, Surigao, *Bolster 342, 249*, May and February, 1906, in forests, 100 to 130 m altitude.

4. Freycinetia luzonensis Presl Epim. Bot. (1851) 238; Warb. in Pflanzenreich 3 (1900) 35; Miq. Fl. Ind. Bat. 3 (1859) 172; Vidal Phan. Cuming. Philip. (1885) 154; Rev. Pl. Vasc. Filip. (1886) 280.

Freycinetia cumingiana Gaudich. Bot. Voy. Bonite (1843) *t. 60 et t. 37, f. 12-14*, sine descr.; C. B. Robinson in Bull. Torr. Bot. Club 35 (1908) 64.

Luzon, Province of Camarines Sur, *Cuming 1455;* Mount Isarog, *For. Bur. 11361 Curran*, May, 1908.

I have examined the number collected by Cuming, cited above, in the Kew and Berlin herbaria, and find that Presl's species is distinct from the form previously determined by me as *F. luzonensis* Presl.[a] It is possible that more than one form is included by Presl in the original description of the species, but this can only be determined by an examination of the material in Presl's herbarium. The specimens I have seen of Cuming's number, seem to agree perfectly with the figure of *F. cumingiana* Gaudich., which, following Warburg, is here considered to be a synonym of *F. luzonensis*. Although the plate representing Gaudichaud's species was published some years earlier than Presl's species, still the description of the plate, but no description of the plant, was not published until 1866 in Charles d' Alleizette's explanation of the plates, 3: 133. Dr. Robinson considered that the *Freycinetia luzonensis* of recent botanists, including Warburg, was different from *F. luzonensis* of Presl, but I am inclined to consider that Warburg correctly interpreted Presl's species, and also correctly reduced to it Gaudichaud's *F. cumingiana*. The material that has been considered as *F. luzonensis* Presl, in this office, and distributed as such, certainly does not represent Presl's species, and is below described as new.

5. Freycinetia vidalii Hemsl. in Kew Bull. (1896) 166; Warb. l. c. 36.

Freycinetia confusa Elm. Leafl. Philip. Bot. 1 (1907) 213; non Ridley, Mater. Fl. Malay Penin. 2 (1907) 233.

Luzon, Province of Nueva Viscaya, Bayombon, *Vidal 3964* in Herb. Kew (type): Province of Tayabas, Lucban, *Elmer 9007*, type of *F. confusa* Elm.

I have examined the type of this species in the Kew Herbarium, and Elmer's *Freycinetia confusa* is manifestly identical. The species belongs in the section *Oligostigma*, although Warburg placed it in the section *Pleiostigma*. The type is an immature specimen, and there is nothing in the original diagnosis from which the proper section can be determined.

6. Freycinetia robinsonii sp. nov. § *Oligostigma*.

Scandens, 2 ad 4 m alta; ramis 1.5 ad 2 cm diametro, ramulis 3 ad 5 mm crassis; foliis submembranaceis, anguste lanceolatis, circiter 20 cm longis, 1 ad 2 cm latis, basi plus minus angustatis vaginantibusque, apice sensim acuminatis, vulgo toto margine et subtus in costis spinulososerratis; inflorescentiis terminalibus, spadicibus femineis 4 vel 5, bracteis multis rubris 6 ad 7 cm longis oblongo-ovatis caudato-acuminatis, acuminibus spinuloso-serratis, exterioribus foliaceis, circumdatis; spadicibus fructiferis cylindraceis, oblongis, 3 ad 5 cm longis, 1 ad 1.5 cm crassis; fructibus circiter 5 mm longis, apice angulato-pyramidatis; stigmatibus 2 vel 3; pedunculis 3 cm longis, scabris.

Luzon, Province of Bataan, Lamao River, *Merrill 3791*, January, 1904; *Williams 338*, December, 1903; *For. Bur. 2194, 2827 Meyer; For. Bur. 752, 2466, 3037* (type) *Borden; Whitford 1311*, June, 1905 and *s. n.*, July, 1904; *Copeland*

---

[a] *Philip. Journ. Sci.* 1 (1906) Suppl. 25.

252, January, 1904: Province of Laguna, Los Baños, *Hallier s. n.*, December, 1903; *Elmer 8242*, April, 1906: Province of Zambales, Mount Abu, *Bur. Sci. 2006 Foxworthy*, December, 1906: Province of Benguet, Sablan, *Elmer 6196*, April, 1904.

A species allied to *Freycinetia luzonensis* Presl, and to *F. multiflora* Merr., differing from the former in its longer leaves, longer and differently shaped syncarps which are more numerous, and from the latter in its shorter, fewer syncarps and shorter leaves. It is the species previously determined by me as *F. luzonensis* Presl.[4]

7. Freycinetia curranii sp. nov. § *Oligostigma*.

Scandens; ramis teretibus, circiter 1.3 cm crassis; foliis numerosis, congestis, coriaceis, nitidis, pallidis, lineari-lanceolatis vel anguste lanceolatis, 40 ad 50 cm longis, 2 ad 3 cm latis, apice sensim longe acuminatis, basi vix angustatis, vaginantibus, marginibus apicem basimque versus spinuloso-dentatis, in media parte inermibus, costa subtus in parte superiore spinuloso-aculeatis. Spadicibus ternis, fructiferis oblongis, cylindraceis, circiter 4 cm longis, 1 ad 1.3 cm crassis; fructibus cylindraceis, angulatis, basi plus minus carnosis, partibus superioribus liberis, 3 mm longis, angulatis, truncatis, stigmatibus 2 vel 3; pedunculis scabridis, 2 cm longis.

LUZON, Province of Camarines, Mount Isarog, *For. Bur. 11359 Curran*, May, 1908, in forests at 1,000 m. alt.

A species allied to *F. auriculata* Merr., but with syncarps less than one-half as long as in that species, the auricles at the base of the leaves membranaceous, and attached to the leaf margin for their entire length, with no free ovate portion.

8. Freycinetia multiflora Merr. in Philip. Journ. Sci. 2 (1907) 259; Elmer Leafl. Philip. Bot. 1 (1907) 213.

LUZON, Province of Tayabas, Lucban, *Elmer 8039, 9009*, May, 1907: Province of Laguna, Mount Maquiling, *For. Bur. 7768 Curran & Merritt*, October, 1907: Province of Rizal, Bosoboso, *For. Bur. 2994 Ahern's collector*, April, 1905; *Bur. Sci. 2092 Ramos*, February, 1907. MINDORO, Mount Halcon, *Merrill 5647*, November, 1906 (type). MINDANAO, Lake Lanao, Camp Keithley, *Mrs. Clemens 73, 1028*, January, 1906, May, 1907; Province of Misamis, Mount Malindang, *For. Bur. 4672 Mearns & Hutchinson*, May, 1906: District of Davao, Mount Apo, *Copeland 1206*, April, 1904.

Closely allied to the preceding, but apparently distinct. *F. luzonensis*, *F. robinsonii*, and *F. multiflora* form a group of allied species, and additional material may lead to a different disposition of some of the specimens cited above.

9. Freycinetia auriculata sp. nov. § *Oligostigma*.

Scandens, robusta, ramulis circiter 1 cm crassis; foliis coriaceis, nitidis, 40 ad 60 cm longis, 1 ad 1.5 cm latis, pallidis, apice sensim attenuato-acuminatis, basi haud angustatis, valde vaginantibus, auriculatis, auriculis 7 ad 10 mm longis, obtusis, coriaceis, marginibus aculeatis, costa subtus in partibus superioribus plus minus aculeatis; inflorescentiis terminalibus, bracteis delapsis; spadicibus ternis, fructiferis cylindraceis,

---

[4] *Philip. Journ. Sci.* 1 (1906) Suppl. 25.

9 ad 11 cm longis, 2 ad 2.5 crassis; fructibus plus minus carnosis, apice liberis, angustatis, 2 mm longis, valde sulcatis, truncatis; stigmatibus 2; pendunculis 5 ad 6 cm longis, minute scabris.

PALAWAN, near Puerto Princesa, *Bur. Sci. 876 Foxworthy*, May, 1906.

10. Freycinetia palawanensis Merr. ex Elm. Leafl. Philip. Bot. 1 (1907-08) 216, 362.

PALAWAN, Victoria Peak, *Bur. Sci. 706 Foxworthy*, March, 1906, alt. 900 m. LUZON, Province of Tayabas, Lucban, *Elmer 7810, 9386*, May, 1907.

11. Freycinetia jagorii Warb. in Pflanzenreich 3 (1900) 39, *f. 10, G.*

SAMAR, *Jagor 954*, in Herb. Berol. (type). MINDANAO, Lake Lanao, Camp Keithley, *Mrs. Clemens s. n.*, September-October, 1906, and March, April, and June, 1907.

The type, which I have examined in the Berlin Herbarium, is an immature specimen, the material collected by Mrs. Clemens being manifestly the same species.

12. Freycinetia philippinensis Hemsl. in Kew Bull. (1896) 165; Warb. l. c. 40.

PHILIPPINES, without locality, *Cuming 1898*, in Herb. Kew. LUZON, Province of Tayabas, *Gregory 117*, August, 1904.

13. Freycinetia rigida Elm. Leafl. Philip. Bot. 1 (1908) 362.

Freycinetia hemsleyi Elm. Leafl. Philip. Bot. 1 (1907) 214; non Warb. in Pflanzenreich 3 (1900) 36.

LUZON, Province of Tayabas, Lucban, *Elmer 7847*, May, 1907.

Manifestly allied to the preceding, but distinct. An immature specimen, *Elmer 6217*, from Sablan, Province of Benguet, Luzon may be referable here.

14. Freycinetia scabripes Warb. in Pflanzenreich 3 (1900) 41.

Freycinetia banahaensis Elm. Leafl. Philip. Bot. 1 (1907) 215.

LUZON, Province of Bataan, *Warburg s. n.*, in Herb. Berol. (type); Lamao River, *For. Bur. 4529 Maule*, May 30, 1906; *For. Bur. 2826 Meyer*, March, 1905: Province of Tayabas, Lucban, *Elmer 7902*, May, 1907, type of *F. banahaensis* Elm. BATAN (Batanes Islands), *Bur. Sci. 3806 Fenix*, June, 1907.

I have examined the type of the species in the Berlin Herbarium, and consider it to be well represented by the specimens from the Lamao River, cited above. The specimen from the Batanes Islands is certainly the same, and I am unable to distinguish Elmer's *F. banahaensis*, a cotype of which is before me.

15. Freycinetia dilatata Merr. ex Elm. Leafl. Philip. Bot. 1 (1907-08) 214, 362.

LUZON, Province of Rizal, near Bosoboso, *Bur. Sci. 99 Foxworthy*, January, 1906; Tanay, *Merrill 2301*, May, 1903: Province of Tayabas, Lucban, *Elmer 9008*, May, 1907.

Plate 437 of the third edition of Blanco's Flora de Filipinas, determined by Naves as *F. luzonensis* var. *heterophylla*, is probably referable here: it is not Presl's variety and certainly is not the same as *F. philippinensis* Hemsl.

16. Freycinetia negrosensis sp. nov. § *Pleiostigma*.

Scandens; foliis dense imbricatis, coriaceis, nitidis, 60 ad 70 cm longis, circiter 2 cm latis, apice longe sensim angustato-acuminatis, basi vix dilatatis ibique in margine membranaceis, toto margine denticulatis, costa subtus minute denticulatis. Spadicibus fructiferis terminalibus, binis vel ternis, densis, oblongis, cylindraceis, 7 ad 10 cm longis, 1.5 cm diametro; fructibus circiter 5 mm longis, plus minus angulatis, apice truncatis; stigmatibus 5 vel 6.

NEGROS, Mount Silay, *Whitford 1541*, May, 1906, in forests on exposed ridges at an altitude of about 1,200 m.

This species is allied to the preceding, and in the preliminary work on the present paper it was considered to be the same as *F. dilatata*. On going over the material with Mr. Elmer, however, it was found that the present species differed constantly from the preceding in its leaves being densely imbricated but not dilated at the base, the membranaceous margins narrower and attached along one side, leaving no free portion at the apex, and by its very dense syncarps and shorter fruits. It has again been collected by Mr. Elmer in southern Negros.

17. **Freycinetia merrillii** Elm. Leafl. Philip. Bot. 1 (1907) 216.

LUZON, Province of Tayabas, Lucban, *Elmer 9101*, May, 1907, type.

18. **Freycinetia megacarpa** sp. nov. § *Pleiostigma*.

Scandens, ramis ramulisque plus minus triangularibus, 5 ad 10 mm crassis, rubro-brunneis; foliis oblongis vel oblongo-lanceolatis, 14 ad 17 cm longis, 3.5 ad 4 cm latis, submembranaceis, apice breviter acuminatis, basi angustatis, vix vaginantibus, margine apicem versus pauce obscureque denticulatis, inferne integris; inflorescentiis terminalibus, ternis vel quaternis; pedunculis 2 ad 3.5 cm longis; syncarpiis globosis vel ovoideis, 3 ad 5 cm diametro; fructibus carnosis, ovoideis vel obovoideis, usque ad 1.5 cm longis, apice plus minus pyramidatis, angulatis, breviter rostratis; stigmatibus circiter 6.

MINDANAO, Lake Lanao, Camp Keithley, *Mrs. Clemens s. n.*, March, 1907.

A species manifestly allied to the preceding, but the leaves lacking the prominent basal auricles, and the margins of the leaves in the basal portions entire or subentire.

19. **Freycinetia monocephala** Elm. Leafl. Philip. Bot. 1 (1906-7) 78, 218.

LUZON, Province of Tayabas, Lucban, and Mount Banajao, *Elmer 7380, 9012*, May, 1907; *Whitford 971*, October, 1904.

A species well characterized by its usually solitary syncarps and very narrow grass-like leaves.

20. **Freycinetia sphaerocephala** Gaudich. Bot. Voy. Bonite (1843) *t. 52*; Warb. in Pflanzenreich 3 (1900) 35.

Freycinetia globosa Merr. in Philip. Journ. Sci. 2 (1907) 260; Elm. Leafl. Philip. Bot. 1 (1907) 217.

Freycinetia strobilacea Vid. Phan. Cuming. Philip. (1885) 154; Rev. Pl. Vasc. Filip. (1886) 280, non Blume.

LUZON, Province of Albay, *Cuming 839*. MINDORO, Mount Halcon, *Merrill 5791*, November, 1906.

Cuming's specimen is probably the type of the species, although Gaudichaud may have collected the same form in the Philippines. A fragment of *Cuming 839* is now in our herbarium, and from the material now available, I find that the differential characters by which *F. globosa* was separated are of no value. The figure of *F. strobilacea* given by Vidal in his Sinopsis Atlas *t. 95, f. B*, was copied from Blume's Rumphia, fide Vidal, l. c. XLII.

21. **Freycinetia rostrata** Merr. in Philip. Journ. Sci. **1** (1906) Suppl. 177.

MINDANAO, Lake Lanao, Camp Keithley, *Mrs. Clemens 475*, April, 1906, and without numbers, July, September, October, 1906, April and June, 1907. SAMAR, Lanang, *Merrill 5235*, October, 1906.

22. **Freycinetia warburgii** Elm. Leafl. Philip. Bot. **1** (1907) 218.

LUZON, Province of Tayabas, Lucban, *Elmer 8229*, May, 1907.

A species with the general appearance of *F. luzonensis* Warb., and *F. robinsonii* Merr., but with less acuminate leaves and manifestly in the section *Pleiostigma*.

23. **Freycinetia ensifolia** Merr. in Govt. Lab. Publ. (Philip.) **17** (1904) 5; Philip. Journ. Sci. **1** (1906) Suppl. 25.

LUZON, Province of Bataan, Mount Mariveles, *Merrill 3242*, October, 1903; *Whitford 329*. May, 1904; *For. Bur. 2624 Meyer*, February, 1905; *Topping 468*; *Elmer 6840*, November, 1904; *For. Bur. 6285 Curran*, February, 1907: Province of Pampanga, Mount Abu, *Bur. Sci. 1944 Foxworthy*, December, 1906.

A local species, common on exposed forested ridges on Mount Mariveles, above 1,000 m altitude.

24. **Freycinetia williamsii** sp. nov. § *Pleiostigma*.

Differt a *F. ensifolia* foliis multo longioribus, sensim tenuiter acuminatis, usque ad 20 cm longis, 7 ad 10 mm latis; syncarpiis multo majoribus, binis vel ternis, rariter solitariis, globosis vel ellipsoideis, 2 ad 3 cm longis latisque.

BATAN (Batanes Islands), Santo Domingo de Basco, *Bur. Sci. 3786 Fenix* (type), June, 1907. LUZON, Province of Benguet, *Bur. Sci. 3504 Mearns*, July, 1907; *Elmer 5857*, March, 1904; *Dr. Pond*, March, 1904; *Williams 1013*, October, 1904: Province of Laguna, Mount Banajao, *Bur. Sci. 6075 Robinson*, March, 1908; Mount Maquiling, *For. Bur. 7706 Curran & Merritt*, October, 1907: Province of Rizal, Bosoboso, *For. Bur. 2696 Ahern's collector*, January–March, 1905.

THE OAKS OF THE PHILIPPINES.

By ELMER D. MERRILL.

(From the Botanical Section of the Biological Laboratory, Bureau of Science, Manila, P. I.)

The first mention of Philippine oaks is in the first edition of Blanco's Flora de Filipinas, in 1837, where three species of *Quercus* are described, and one species of *Castanopsis*, the latter as a *Fagus* and without specific name. The three true oaks, Blanco identified with extra-Philippine species, one as *Quercus molucca* Rumph., of eastern Malaya, one with *Q. glabra* presumably of Thunberg, and one with *Q. cerris* Linn., an European species. In the second edition of the work, the name *Quercus molucca* is changed to *Q. concentrica*, *Q. glabra* is changed to *Q. ovalis*, and a short description of a fourth species, *Q. cooperta*, is added. The identification of these species has caused considerable confusion, and one of the objects of the present paper is to determine their status, so far as possible.

Nothing further appeared regarding Philippine *Quercus* until A. De Candolle's monograph of the family in 1864,[1] when *Quercus llanosii* A. DC., based on specimens supplied by Father Llanos, supposed to represent Blanco's *Quercus concentrica*, and *Q. philippinensis* A. DC., based on a specimen collected in Luzon by Cuming, were described. *Quercus ovalis* Blanco was admitted, with a short diagnosis taken from Blanco's description, while the new name *Q. blancoi* was proposed for Blanco's *Q. glabra*, the author overlooking the fact that in publishing *Quercus ovalis*, Blanco simply proposed a new name for his own *Q. glabra*. *Q. cooperta* Blanco is also included but with doubt as to whether or not it was a true *Quercus*, while a drawing sent by Llanos was identified as probably *Quercus pruinosa* Blume, although so far this species has not been found in the Philippines.

In 1875, Máximo Laguna y Villanueva published in Madrid, a pamphlet of eight pages,[2] with one plate, enumerating the species of *Quercus* previously recorded from the Philippines, and described and figured

---

[1] Prodr. 16² (1864) 1–123.

[2] Apuntes sobre un nuevo roble (Q. jordanae) de la flora de Filipinas. (1875) 1–8, cum lamina.

Quercus jordanae as a new species, the type material being from the Caraballo Mountains in Central Luzon.

In 1883, F.-Villar [3] credited nineteen species of *Quercus* to the Philippines, two of which were described as new. It is evident that nearly all of these were admitted on erroneous identifications. Many of them it will be quite impossible to identify, but some were cleared up by Vidal.[4]

In 1883, Vidal [5] figured no less than seven species of *Quercus* and two species of *Castanopsis,* two of the former being described as new, while in 1886 ten species of *Quercus* and one *Castanopsis* are enumerated by him [6] with specific names, and two species of *Quercus* and one *Castanopsis* without specific names. Two species of *Quercus* are described as new, while the descriptions of *Q. vidalii* F.-Vill., and *Q. blancoi* A. DC., are amplified.

Wenzig's paper on "Die Eichen Ost- und Südasiens" [7] adds nothing to our knowledge of Philippine oaks, a single species, *Quercus philippinensis* A. DC., being credited to the Philippines, *Q. llanosii. Q. ovalis* Blanco, and *Q. blancoi* A. DC., being erroneously reduced to it.

King's valuable paper "The Indo-Malayan Species of Quercus and Castanopsis" [8] does not include the Philippine species, but is the one most useful work in determining the Philippine species of this group.

Six species of *Quercus* are enumerated from the Philippines by Von Seemen,[9] and a single one was described by Hance.

Our Philippine oaks are difficult to determine properly, chiefly because of lack of complete material, and because many of the species were originally described from immature specimens. After an examination of Vidal's types at Kew, some of Blume's types at Leiden, and the types of DeCandolle's Philippine species at Geneva, I was impressed with the discrepancies in the identifications of the Philippine species, and on my return to Manila considered it advisable to examine critically the entire material available, and publish an enumeration of the species. Most of the specimens cited by Vidal I found at Kew, but some of the numbers do not appear to be extant, and while there I succeeded in matching most of Vidal's species with recently collected specimens, although if Vidal's specimens were now before me, I have no doubt but that the present paper would be more accurate, so far as the disposition of his species is concerned.

It is frequently difficult to accurately identify specimens unless they have mature fruits, and for this reason, it is to be expected that some of

[3] Nov. App. (1883) 207–209.
[4] Rev. Pl. Vasc. Filip. (1886) 260–265.
[5] Sinopsis Atlas (1883) XLI. t. 92.
[6] Rev. Pl. Vasc. Filip. (1886) 260–265.
[7] Jahrb. Kgl. Bot. Gart. Berlin 4 (1886) 214–240.
[8] Ann. Bot. Gard. Calcutta 2 (1889) 17–107, pl. 15–104.
[9] Perkins Frag. Fl. Philip. (1904) 41, 42.

the specimens referred to definite species below will later be found to be really different, when additional material is secured. I have below disposed the specimens in flower, and those with immature fruits, to the best of my ability, but am not always sure that they are always correctly referred. Although a great number of specimens have been cited, the following paper by no means accounts for all in our herbarium, for I have described no new species excepting those of which mature fruits were available. It is apparent that several forms remain to be described at a later date when more complete material is secured.

Most of the species of *Quercus* found in the Philippines are endemic, but four species, as here interpreted, being found outside of the Philippines, two in Celebes, *Quercus llanosii* and *Q. ovalis,* if the identification of the Celebes material is correct, and two, *Q. reflexa* King and *Q. bennettii* Miq., in Borneo, the latter extending to Bangka and Malacca.

Nearly all our species of the genus are found in the hill or mountain forests at medium and higher altitudes, but three species being known from comparatively low altitudes, *Q. caudatifolia,* occuring at least as low as 20 m above sea level in Mindanao, and *Q. bennettii* and *Q. soleriana,* being found as low as 100 m on Mount Mariveles, in Luzon. Some species, like *Quercus jordanae,* are very abundant in the mossy forests like those of Mount Data and Mount Tonglon, at altitudes as high as 2,250 m, but the great bulk of the species are found at altitudes of from 400 to 1,500 m.

KEY TO THE PHILIPPINE GENERA AND SPECIES OF FAGACEÆ.

Involucre inclosing the nuts, often splitting irregularly, armed externally with rather long spines, usually containing more than one nut............ 1. *Castanopsis*
Involucre inclosing the nut in few species only, mostly cup- or saucer-shaped, covered with imbricate scales, or zonulate, rarely tuberculate, never containing more than one nut... 2. *Quercus*

1. CASTANOPSIS Spach.

1. **Castanopsis philippensis** (Blanco) Vidal Rev. Pl. Vasc. Filip. (1886) 265. (*philippinensis*).

Fagus philippensis Blanco Fl. Filip. ed. 2 (1845) 503, err. typ. *philipensis*.
Castanopsis sumatrana F.-Vill. Nov. App. (1883) 210, fide Vidal, non A. DC.
Castanopsis javanica Vidal Sinopsis Atlas (1883) t. 92, f. I, non A. DC.

LUZON, Province of Rizal, Bosoboso, *Bur. Sci. 2658 Ramos*, May, 1907; *For. Bur. 2148, 2872, 3100 Ahern's collector*, November, 1904, March, May, 1905. MINDORO, Calausan, *For. Bur. 8547 Merritt*, January, 1908.

The specimens cited above agree with *Vidal 611bis,* in Herb. Kew. collected at Angat, Province of Bulacan, Luzon, and also agree with Blanco's description. Endemic.

A second species, probably undescribed, occurs in the Philippines, enumerated by Vidal l. c., as *Castanopsis* sp., and previously erroneously identified by F.-Villar l. c., as *C. javanica* A. DC., and by Vidal, Sinopsis Atlas l. c., *f. H,* as *C. sumatrana.* I have no specimens of it.

2. QUERCUS Linn.

Involucres cup-shaped, saucer-shaped, or discoid, their bracts imbricate, free or united by their bases only, the apices always free............................ § PASANIA
  Leaves more or less pubescent or puberulent beneath.
    Leaves subcoriaceous, slightly pubescent beneath, at least along the midrib and lateral nerves, the reticulations lax, very distinct........ 1. *Q. clementis*
    Leaves firmly coriaceous, densely and uniformly ferruginous-pubescent beneath, the reticulations obscure................................ 2. *Q. jordanae*
  Leaves entirely glabrous beneath, or at most minutely puberulent.
    Leaves mostly exceeding 12 cm in length............................. 3. *Q. llanosii*
    Leaves 4 to 6 cm long............................. 4. *Q. luzoniensis*
Involucres cup-shaped, their bracts connate into entire or denticulate concentric lamellæ .... § CYCLOBALANUS
  Glans manifestly longer than broad.
    Leaves more or less pubescent or puberulent beneath; glans never more than 12 mm in diameter............................. 5. *Q. caudatifolia*
    Leaves entirely glabrous beneath, glans exceeding 12 mm in diameter.
      Glans at least 2 cm in diameter............................. 6. *Q. merrittii*
      Glans about 1.5 cm in diameter............................. 7. *Q. ovalis*
  Glans at least as broad as long, frequently broader than long.
    Leaves 8 to 11 cm wide.
      Involucres inclosing less than one-third the glans; leaf-margins sometimes somewhat repand above............................. 8. *Q. woodii*
      Involucres inclosing about three-fourths the glans; leaf-margins entire.
        9. *Q. castellarnauiana*
    Leaves 7 cm wide or less.
      Leaves more than 6 cm long, strongly acuminate, entire.
        Lamellæ of the involucre 5 to 8, usually denticulate.
          Leaves densely cinereous-ferruginous-puberulent beneath.
            10. *Q. acuminatissima*
          Leaves glabrous beneath.
            Leaves usually abruptly acuminate.
              Leaves 7 to 15 cm long; reticulations on the lower surface fine but evident .... 11. *Q. soleriana*
              Leaves 12 to 25 cm long; reticulations on the lower surface obsolete .... 9. *Q. castellarnauiana*
            Leaves gradually and slenderly caudate-acuminate, 6 to 8 cm long .... 12. *Q. philippinensis*
        Lamellæ of the involucre 3 or 4, obscurely denticulate; leaves abruptly short-acuminate, the acumen blunt............................. 13. *Q. bennettii*
      Leaves 5 cm long or less, acute, obtuse, or very obscurely acuminate, the margins sometimes slightly sinuate above............................. 14. *Q. merrillii*
Involucres ovoid, externally tubercular, closed and inclosing the whole glans but not adnate to it except at the base............................. § CHLAMYDOBALANUS
  Leaves with about 15 pairs of lateral nerves............................. 15. *Q. cooperta*
  Leaves with 10 to 12 pairs of lateral nerves............................. 16. *Q. reflexa*
Involucres large, thick, woody, turbinate, the upper portion tubercled, nearly enveloping the glans and adherent to it on the base and sides; glans bony.
        § LITHOCARPUS
  Leaves somewhat pubescent beneath, the branchlets densely ferruginous-villous; involucre 3 cm in diameter............................. 17. *Q. curranii*

§ PASANIA.

1. Quercus clementis sp. nov.

Arbor 10 ad 13 m alta, inflorescentiis, subtus foliis, ramulisque plus minus ferrugineo-pubescentibus; foliis oblongis vel elliptico-oblongis, rigide chartaceis vel subcoriaceis, 10 ad 18 cm longis, basi acutis, apice breviter obtuseque acuminatis, integris, nitidis, subtus sparse pubescentibus, reticulis laxis, distinctis; cupulis 2 ad 2.5 cm diametro, utrinque dense ferrugineo-pubescentibus; glandibus subcylindraceis, apice subtruncatis, 2 cm longis.

A tree 10 to 13 m high, the branchlets and inflorescence densely ferruginous-pubescent. Branches slender, reddish-brown, ultimately glabrous. Leaves alternate, oblong or elliptical-oblong, 10 to 18 cm long, 4 to 7 cm wide, firmly chartaceous or subcoriaceous, the base acute, the apex rather abruptly and shortly acuminate, the acumen blunt, margins entire, slightly recurved, shining on both surfaces, the upper surface glabrous, or pubescent on the midrib and lateral nerves, the lower surface more or less pubescent on the midrib and nerves, and with scattered hairs on the surface, in age nearly glabrous; lateral nerves 10 to 12 on each side of the midrib, strongly impressed on the upper surface, very prominent beneath, anastomosing and forming a somewhat arched submarginal nerve, the reticulations rather lax, very distinct; petioles stout, more or less pubescent, 5 mm long. Male inflorescence: spikes 8 to 13 cm long, fascicled in the upper axils or in depauperate panicles, densely ferruginous-pubescent; flowers sessile, solitary, the perianth 2 mm long, densely pubescent, 6-lobed; stamens 10, the longer filaments 3 mm. Female inflorescence: spikes 12 to 20 cm long, in terminal panicles, when young densely pubescent, in age subglabrous; flowers solitary, numerous, pubescent. Fruits maturing the second year, the involucres 1 cm high or less, 2 to 2.5 cm in diameter, densely ferruginous-pubescent on both surfaces, the scales on the outer surface very numerous, appressed, imbricate, acuminate, about 2 mm long. Glans 2 cm long and 2 cm in diameter, deciduous-puberulent, subcylindrical, the sides parallel, the apex very abruptly rounded-subtruncate, apiculate.

MINDANAO, Lake Lanao, Camp Keithley, *Mrs. Clemens 906*, February, 1907, and four sheets without numbers from the same locality, April, June, and September, 1907. A closely allied form is represented by *Clemens 1138*, from the same locality, but the specimen has immature fruits and its leaves have about 15 pairs of lateral nerves.

The species above described seems to be allied to *Quercus lamponga* Miq., of the Malayan region, but is apparently sufficiently distinct from that species, the scales of the involucre not arranged in lamellæ. It is well characterized by its subcylindrical glans that is as long as broad, and its rather laxly and strongly reticulate leaves. According to the collector the bark of this tree peels off in thin papery flakes similar to that of many species of *Betula*.

2. **Quercus jordanae** Laguna Apuntes Sobre Nuev. Roble de Filip. (1875) 7, *cum lamina;* F.-Vill. Nov. App. (1883) 208; Vid. Rev. Pl. Vasc. Filip. (1886) 264; Ceron Cat. Pl. Herb. (1892) 165.

Q. vidalii F.-Vill. Nov. App. (1883) 209; Vidal Sinopsis Atlas XLI (1883) t. 92, f. B.; Ceron Cat. Pl. Herb. (1892) 164.

Q. caraballoana F.-Vill. Nov. App. (1883) 209; Vidal l. c. 265; Ceron l. c. 165.

Q. havilandii Von Seem. in Perk. Frag. Fl. Philip. (1904) 42, non Stapf.

Q. sundaica Merr. in Philip. Journ. Sci. 1 (1906) Suppl. 41, non Blume.

LUZON, District of Lepanto, Mount Data, *Merrill 4550*, November, 1905; *Loher 4873*: Province of Benguet, Pauai, *Bur. Sci. 4407, 4480 Mearns*, August, 1907; Mount Tonglon (Santo Tomas), *Williams 1321, 1365*, October, 1904; *For. Bur. 5009 Curran*, August, 1906; Baguio, *Lardizabal 7*, 1901: Province of Bataan, Mount Mariveles, *For. Bur. 1253 Borden*, July, 1904; *Whitford 1186*, March, 1905: Province of Tayabas, Mount Banajao, *For. Bur. 7912 Curran & Merritt*, November, 1907; *Elmer 7903*, May, 1907.

Quercus jordanae Laguna, as here interpreted, is a rather variable species, but after examining the above series of specimens I have concluded that all are referable to one species. *Q. jordanae* was placed by its author in the section *Cyclobalanus*, but all the specimens cited above are manifestly of the section *Pasania*. The species as figured by Laguna has relatively broader leaves than has *Quercus vidalii* as figured by Vidal, but the indumentum seems to be nearly the same in both, as well as the shape of the base and apex of the leaves, and the venation. I have seen the type number of *Quercus vidalii* in Herb. Kew (*Vidal 617 bis*), and it is well matched by the specimens from Mount Mariveles, cited above. His specimen was from the same region as the type of *Quercus jordanae*, the Caraballo Mountains, in central Luzon. The specimens from Lepanto and Benguet differ from those of Mount Mariveles and Mount Banajao in having somewhat more coriaceous and slightly more pubescent leaves, and rather more pubescent involucres, the scales being also more prominent, but good differential specific characters appear to be lacking. *Vidal 1814*, in Herb. Kew, which was mentioned by Stapf in the original description of *Quercus havilandii*[10] as possibly referable to the Bornean species, is almost certainly referable to the species here considered as *Q. jordanae*, but the specimen is without flowers and fruit, so that its absolute identification will always be more or less doubtful. I do not consider it to be the same as *Q. havilandii*. *Quercus caraballoana* F.-Vill., to which Vidal refers his No. 618bis, is surely the same as *Q. jordanae* (*Q. vidalii*), although the specimen does not appear to be extant, as I could not find it in the Kew herbarium. F.-Villar's description however applies very closely to the specimens above cited, while Vidal[11] states that it appeared to him to be very close to Laguna's species, giving only some trivial characters by which it could be distinguished. *Quercus sundaica* Bl., was admitted by me[12] on the strength of identifications made by O. Von Seemen, but Blume's species is quite different, its leaves having about 15 pairs of lateral nerves, while *Q. jordanae* has but 9 or 10 pairs. A specimen in the U. S. National Herbarium, *Lardizabal 7*, was identified at Berlin as *Quercus pruinosa* Blume, but this is a manifest error, as *Q. pruinosa* has quite different fruits, and differs from *Q. jordanae* in many other characters. The specimen determined by Von Seemen as *Quercus havilandii*,[13] *Loher 4873*, is not Stapf's species, but is the same as the other specimens from Lepanto and Benguet here referred to *Q. jordanae*.

[10] Trans. Linn. Soc. Bot. II 4 (1894) 231, pl. 18, f. A.
[11] Rev. Pl. Vasc. Filip. (1886) 265.
[12] *This Journal* 1 (1906) Suppl. 41.
[13] Perk. Frag. Fl. Philip. (1904) 42.

3. Quercus llanosii A. DC. Prodr. 16 ² (1864) 97, excl. syn. Blanco.

Q. companoana Vidal Sinopsis Atlas (1883) XLI, *t. 92, f. D;* Rev. Pl. Vasc. Filip. (1886) 260; Ceron Cat. Pl. Herb. (1892) 164; Koord. Meded. 's Lands Plantent. **19** (1898) 615 ?

Q. sundaica F.-Vill. Nov. App. (1883) 207, excl. syn. Naves, fide Vidal; non Blume.

LUZON, without locality, *Llanos* in Herb. DeCandolle (type): Province of Cagayan, San Vicente, *For. Bur. 7086 Klemme*, May, 1907: Province of Rizal, Bosoboso, *Merrill 3680*, June, 1903; *Bur. Sci. 2100 Ramos*, February, 1907; Tanay, *Merrill 2344*, May, 1903: Province of Bataan, Lamao River, *For. Bur. 7368 Curran*, July, 1907. Local names *Maculab, Manloab, Bayucan, Catiban, Pagnan.*

I have examined the type of this species in the DeCandolle Herbarium, and also the type number of *Quercus companoana* Vidal at Kew, and although the type of *Quercus llanosii* is a flowering specimen with leaves 20 cm in length, and the type of *Q. companoana* is a specimen with immature fruits and with leaves 8 to 13 cm in length, I am disposed to consider the two species identical, and accordingly here reduce Vidal's species. The account of the fruit and Blanco's synonyms must be excluded from DeCandolle's description of the species, as *Quercus concentrica* Blanco appears to be referable to *Q. soleriana*. This may be the species determined by Blanco as *Quercus cerris*, as suggested by Vidal. Koorders has reported this species from Celebes, under *Q. companoana* Vidal.

4. Quercus luzoniensis sp. nov.

Arbuscula vel arbor parva subglabra; ramis teretibus, lenticellatis, ramulis glabris, nigricantibus; foliis alternis, coriaceis, integris, 4 ad 6 cm longis, oblongo-lanceolatis vel elliptico-lanceolatis, breviter acuminatis, basi acutis, supra nitidis, subtus glabris vel minutissime griseo-puberulis; cupulis circiter 1 cm diametro, utrinque cinereo-pubescentibus, squamulis imbricatis, acuminatis, adpressis, circiter 1.5 mm longis; glandibus conico-ovoideis, glabris, nitidis, apiculatis, circiter 1 cm altis crassisque.

A shrub or small tree about 6 m high, nearly glabrous. Branches terete, lenticellate, brownish, the branchlets somewhat angled, slender, glabrous, blackish when dry. Leaves alternate, oblong-lanceolate to elliptical-lanceolate, 4 to 6 cm long, 1.5 to 2.5 cm wide, the apex rather gradually short-acuminate, the base acute or slightly decurrent-acuminate, the margins entire, recurved, coriaceous, the upper surface glabrous, shining, the lower surface slightly paler, dull, glabrous or very minutely grayish-puberulent; nerves about 7 on each side of the midrib, obsolete or nearly so above, distinct beneath, the reticulations obsolete or nearly so; petioles about 5 mm long. Inflorescence unknown. Fruits in short spikes, terminal or in the upper axils; involucre about 7 mm high, abruptly narrowed below into a stout stalk, about 1 cm in diameter, rather densely gray-pubescent on both surfaces, the scales lanceolate, acuminate, alternate, imbricate, not arranged in concentric lines; glans ovoid-conical, glabrous, shining, about 1 cm high and the same in diameter, apiculate.

LUZON, Province of Benguet, Mount Tonglon, *For. Bur. 5040 Curran*, August, 1906 (type); Pauai, *Bur. Sci. 4411 Mearns*, July, 1907, sterile: Province of Zambales, Mount Tapulao, *For. Bur. 8081 Curran & Merritt*, December, 1907, sterile.

A species well characterized by its small coriaceous leaves and small fruits, the involucres being rather densely cinereous-pubescent. In leaf characters somewhat similar to *Quercus merrillii* Von Seem., but the fruits are entirely different.

§ CYCLOBALANUS.

5. Quercus caudatifolia sp. nov.

Arbor 17 ad 25 m alta; foliis oblongo-lanceolatis, 8 ad 14 cm longis, basi acutis, apice sensim caudato-acuminatis, acuminibus obtusis, supra glabris, subtus pallidioribus, junioribus plus minus cinereo-ferrugineo-puberulis, nervis utrinque circiter 10, subtus distinctis, reticulis subobsoletis; glandibus oblongo-conico-ovoideis, puberulis, 1.5 ad 2 cm longis, 8 ad 12 mm diametro; cupulis plus minus cinereo- vel ferrugineo-puberulis, circiter 7 mm altis.

A tree 17 to 25 m high. Branches terete, slender, ultimately glabrous, sparingly lenticellate, dark-reddish-brown to nearly black, the branchlets rather densely ferruginous-pubescent. Leaves alternate, oblong-lanceolate, subcoriaceous, 8 to 14 cm long, 2.5 to 4 cm wide, the base acute, the apex gradually narrowed to the rather slender, caudate, blunt acumen, the margins entire, the upper surface shining, glabrous, or when young very slightly pubescent, the lower surface paler, when young more or less ferruginous-cinereous-puberulent, especially along the midrib and nerves, apparently glabrous in age or nearly so; nerves about 10 on each side of the midrib, distinct beneath, obscurely anastomosing, the reticulations indistinct, nearly obsolete; petioles 5 to 10 mm long, usually pubescent. Female flowers spicately disposed, the spikes fascicled in the upper axils or arranged in terminal 5 to 7 cm long, panicles, ferruginous-pubescent. Glans oblong-conical-ovoid, 1.5 to 2 cm long, more or less puberulent, apiculate, 8 mm in diameter in the type, in other specimens 9 to 12 mm in diameter below. Cup about 7 mm high, including the thickened stipe, 10 to 12 mm in diameter, inclosing only the base of the glans, more or less ferruginous- or cinereous-pubescent outside, nearly glabrous within, the laminæ about 7, concentric, denticulate, the teeth very short, acute.

Type specimen from Lamao River, Mount Mariveles, Province of Bataan, Luzon, *For. Bur. 806 Borden*, May, 1904, at an altitude of about 700 m. I am disposed to refer here also the following specimens; *Elmer 6897*, November, 1904; *Whitford 276*, May, 1904, from the same locality: Province of Ilocos Sur, La Paz, *For. Bur. 5668 Klemme*, October, 1906: Province of Zambales, Botolan, *Merrill 2979*, June, 1903: Province of Rizal, Bosoboso, *Merrill 2702*, June, 1903: Province of Pangasinan, *For. Bur. 8277 Curran & Merritt*, December, 1907: Province of Camarines, *For. Bur. 10644 Curran*, June, 1908.

The species as here described is the Mariveles form, and some of the other specimens referred to it differ in some minor characters, in some specimens (*Curran 10644*), the leaves being quite glabrous. It is well characterized by its small fruits, which are considerably longer than thick. The species figured by Vidal in his Sinopsis, Atlas, *t. 92, f. A.*, as doubtfully representing *Quercus celebica* Miq., is probably referable here. It is certainly not Miquel's species. Local names: T., *Catabang, Bayucan;* Il., *Diraan, Dalutan*.

6. Quercus merrittii sp. nov.

Arbor circiter 18 m alta, glabra; foliis elliptico-lanceolatis, papyraceis, utrinque acuminatis, circiter 15 cm longis, integris, nitidis, nervis utrinque 9, subtus prominentibus, reticulis minutis, densis; glandibus conico-ovoideis, minute cinereo-puberulis, apiculatis, basi convexis, circiter 3 cm longis, 2 ad 2.2 cm diametro; cupulis 1.5 cm altis.

A tree about 18 m high, glabrous. Branchlets slender, terete or slightly angled, sparingly lenticellate, gray or reddish-brown. Leaves alternate, papyraceous, 13 to 15 cm long, 3.5 to 5 cm broad, the base somewhat decurrent-acuminate, the apex rather strongly caudate-acuminate, the acumen about 2 cm long, blunt, the margins entire, both surfaces rather pale when dry, somewhat shining; nerves 9 on each side of the midrib, prominent beneath, ascending, somewhat curved and very obscurely anastomosing, the reticulations very fine, dense, not prominent; petioles about 1 cm long. Flowers unknown. Glans conical-ovoid, minutely and deciduously cinereous-puberulent outside, the apex apiculate, the base convex, about 3 cm long, 2 to 2.2 cm in diameter; cup inclosing the basal fourth of the glans, including the stout stipe about 1.5 cm high, glabrous, or the outside minutely puberulent, the laminæ indistinct, 6 or 7, denticulate, the teeth very short.

LUZON, Province of Tayabas, Mount Banajao, *For. Bur. 8047 Curran & Merritt*, November, 1907, altitude 700 m.

This species is well characterized by its large fruits, its acorns being considerably larger than those of any other species known from the Philippines.

7. Quercus ovalis Blanco

Fl. Filip. ed. 2 (1845) 502; A. DC. Prodr. 16^2 (1864) 97; F.-Vill. Nov. App. (1883) 208, *cum descript.!;* Vidal Rev. Pl. Vasc. Filip. (1886) 262; Ceron Cat. Pl. Herb. (1892) 164.

Q. glabra Blanco Fl. Filip. (1837) 727, non Thunb.

Q. blancoi A. DC. Prodr. 16^2 (1864) 97; Vidal Cat. Pl. Prov. Manila (1880) 42; Sinopsis Atlas (1883) XLI, *t. 92, f. C;* Rev. Pl. Vasc. Filip. (1886) 262, *cum descript.!;* Ceron Cat. Pl. Herb. (1892) 164; Koord. Meded. 's Lands Plantent. 19 (1898) 615.

Q. induta F.-Vill. Nov. App. (1883) 207, fide Vidal, non Blume.

Q. teysmanni F.-Vill. l. c., fide Vidal, non Blume.

LUZON, Province of Zambales, *For. Bur. 5817 Curran*, January, 1907: Province of Pampanga, Mount Abu, *Bur. Sci. 1909 Foxworthy*, January, 1907: Province of Bulacan, Angat, *For. Bur. 3235 Russell*, June, 1905: Province of Rizal, Bosoboso, *For. Bur. 10017 Curran*, February, 1908: Province of Batangas, Mount Malaraya, *For. Bur. 7847 Curran & Merritt*, November, 1907.

A very characteristic species, entirely glabrous or nearly so, with shining coriaceous leaves. Blanco's specific name *ovalis* is the earliest valid one available, and is here retained. *Quercus blancoi* A. DC., was based on *Q. glabra* Blanco, non Thunb., but *Q. ovalis* of the second edition of the Flora de Filipinas is manifestly *Q. glabra* of the first edition, Blanco having recognized his own error in referring Philippine material to Thunberg's species, simply proposed the new name *ovalis*, but did not indicate this. Vidal[14] has attempted to hold *Quer-*

---

[14] Rev. Pl. Vasc. Filip. (1886) 262.

cus blancoi and *Q. ovalis* distinct, but this is inadmissable, as *Q. ovalis* and *Q. blancoi* are both only new names of the same species, *Q. glabra* Blanco, non Thunb., and are hence synonyms. I could not find the specimen in Herb. Kew, referred by Vidal to *Q. ovalis* (*Vidal 616bis*), but the specimens referred by him to *Q. blancoi* are identical with those cited above as representing the species. The specimen collected by Russell is a topotype, and was received under the same native name that Blanco cites, and agrees perfectly with his description, so I do not consider that there is the least doubt as to the identity of the species. Local names: T., *Uayan, Malabingao*.

8. Quercus woodii Hance in Journ. Bot. **12** (1874) 240; F.-Vill. Nov. App. (1883) 208.

LUZON, without locality, *Wood*, in Herb. Mus. Brit. (type): Province of Benguet, Baguio, *Williams 949, 980*, June, September, 1904; *Elmer 5900*, March, 1904.

The type of this species, which I have examined in the Herbarium of the British Museum, is very fragmentary, consisting of mature fruits and mere fragments of leaves, showing only the basal portions of two or three leaves. It is closely matched by Williams' specimens cited above. It is closely allied to *Quercus soleriana* Vidal, but has relatively much broader leaves, which are sometimes slightly repand above. Elmer's specimen was determined by Von Seemen as *Quercus pallida* Blume, but is quite unlike Blume's species, the type of which I have examined in Herb. Leiden. The leaves of *Quercus woodii* have but 9 or 10 pairs of lateral nerves, while those of *Q. pallida* Blume have about 15 pairs. Moreover the fruits are quite different, Blume's species being characterized by its very broad and flattened glans. *Q. pallida* is well figured by King in Ann. Bot. Gard. Calcutta **2** (1889) *pl. 534*, and I have seen nothing closely approaching it from the Philippines.

9. Quercus castellarnauiana Vid. Rev. Pl. Vasc. Filip. (1886) 264; Ceron Cat. Pl. Herb. (1892) 165.

The type of this species was from the Island of Marinduque, *Vidal 1806*, locally known as *Puso-puso*. I am not at all sure that it belongs in this section, and it may be a species of the section *Pasania*, and allied to *Q. llanosii* A. DC.

10. Quercus acuminatissima sp. nov.
Quercus celebica Von Seem. in Perk. Frag. Fl. Philip. (1904) 41, non Miq.
Quercus philippinensis Merr. in For. Bur. Bull. **1** (1903) 16, non A. DC.

Arbor mediocriter, inflorescentiis, subtus foliis, ramulisque plus minus dense cinereo-ferrugineo-puberulis vel pubescentibus; foliis late oblongo-lanceolatis, 9 ad 17 cm longis, subcoriaceis, integris, basi acutis vel acuminatis, apice valde tenuiter acuminatis, supra brunneis, nitidis, glabris, subtus pallidioribus; glandibus conico-ovoideis, acuminatis, 1.8 ad 2.2 cm diametro, 1.5 ad 2 cm altis; cupulis extus dense ferrugineo- vel cinereo-pubescentibus, laminibus 8 ad 10, denticulatis.

A medium-sized tree, the branchlets, inflorescence, and lower surface of the leaves rather densely ferruginous- or cinereous-puberulent or pubescent. Branches terete, grayish- or reddish-brown, somewhat lenticellate, rugose, glabrous, the branchlets usually pubescent. Leaves alternate, broadly oblong-lanceolate, subcoriaceous, 9 to 17 cm long, 3 to 4.5 cm wide, entire, the base acute or somewhat acuminate, the apex strongly and slenderly acuminate, the acumen frequently 2 cm long, narrowed upwards to the blunt or acute point, the upper surface brown, shining, glabrous, the lower surface pale and densely ferruginous-cinereous-puberulent; nerves about 9 on each side of the midrib, distinct beneath, the reticulations obsolete; petioles glabrous or pubescent, about 1 cm long. Male inflorescence densely ferruginous-pubescent, in terminal panicles 7 to 15 cm long. Female inflorescence of solitary, axillary, pubescent spikes 7 to 11 cm long, the flowers solitary. Glans conical-ovoid, glabrous, shining, the base truncate, the apex acuminate, apiculate, 1.8 to 2.2 cm in diameter, 1.5 to 2 cm high; cup inclosing only the basal portion of the glans, saucer-shaped, densely ferruginous- or cinereous-puberulent outside, the laminæ 8 to 10, concentric, denticulate, the scales of the lower laminæ quite united, those of the upper less so.

MINDANAO, Province of Surigao, Placer, *Ahern 432*, February–May, 1901 (type) N. v., *Uyayan*. I am disposed to refer here also the following specimens, all from Mindanao: Maria Cristina Falls, *Mrs. Clemens 709*, October, 1906: Lake Lanao, Camp Keithley, *Mrs. Clemens 1176*, September, 1907: District of Zamboanga, Port Banga, *For. Bur. 9066, 9143, 9417 Whitford & Hutchinson*, November, 1907, to February, 1908.

This species was previously identified erroneously by me as *Q. philippinensis* A. DC., to which it is not at all closely allied, and later the same specimen was referred by Von Seemen to *Quercus celebica* Miq. It does not, however, appear to be very closely allied to Miquel's species, which was placed by DeCandolle in the section *Cyclobalanus*, and by King in the section *Pasania*. I am of the opinion that the present species is a *Cyclobalanus*, although the bracts of the upper laminæ are nearly free. It differs decidedly from *Quercus celebica* in being more pubescent, with larger fruits and very much more acuminate leaves. This species grows at lower altitudes than any other species known from the Philippines, occurring in the District of Zamboanga in dipterocarp forests at an altitude of from 20 to 30 m above the sea.

11. **Quercus soleriana** Vidal Rev. Pl. Vasc. Filip. (1886) 261; Ceron Cat. Pl. Herb. (1892) 164.

Quercus concentrica Blanco Fl. Filip. ed. 2 (1845) 502, non Lour.

Quercus molucca Blanco Fl. Filip. (1837) 726, non Rumph.

Quercus reinwardtii F.-Vill. Nov. App. (1883) 207, fide Vidal, non Korth.

Quercus costata var. *convexa* Naves Fl. Filip. ed. 3, *t. 441*, non Blume.

Quercus clementiana Merr. in Philip. Journ. Sci. 1 (1906) Suppl. 41, non King.

Quercus llanosii Merr. in Philip. Journ. Sci. 2 (1907) 270, non A. DC.

LUZON, Province of Benguet, Twin Peaks, *Elmer 6443*, June, 1904: Province of Zambales, *For. Bur. 6811 Curran*, May, 1907: Province of Bulacan, Angat, *For. Bur. 11154 Aguilar*, April, 1908: Province of Rizal, Bosoboso, *For. Bur. 1148, 3258 Ahern's collector*, June, 1904, August, 1905; *Bur. Sci. 4659 Ramos*, August, 1907: Province of Batangas, *For. Bur. 7664 Curran & Merritt*, October, 1907: Province of Laguna, Santa Maria Mavitac, *For. Bur. 10101 Curran*, February, 1908: Province of Bataan, Mount Mariveles, *Elmer 6898*, November, 1904; *For. Bur. 2997 Meyer*, May, 1905; *Whitford 1178, 1180*, March, 1905; *For. Bur. 5458 Curran*, November, 1906; *Bur. Sci. 1598 Foxworthy*, October, 1906: Province of Tayabas, Unisan, *For. Bur. 1824, 1825 Klemme*, September, 1904. MINDORO, Mount Halcon, *Merrill 5695*, November, 1906; Mount Malasumbu, *For. Bur. 8586*,

8749 Merritt, January, 1908; Mount Inauan, *For. Bur. 8721 Merritt*, January, 1908. MINDANAO, District of Davao, Todaya and Mount Apo, *Williams 2608, 3035*, April, July, 1905; *Copeland 1145, 1271*, April, 1904.

By far the most common and widely distributed species of the genus in the Philippines, and rather variable. Vidal's type is minutely matched by *Elmer 6443*, and by the specimens from Rizal Province cited above. *Quercus concentrica* Blanco non Lour., and *Q. molucca* Blanco non Rumph., are referred here, as Blanco's descriptions apply closely to the present species. *Quercus clementiana* was admitted by me on the strength of identifications made by Von Seemen, but an examination of authentic material of King's species, shows that it is distinct from *Q. soleriana*. The mature glans is about 2 cm long, and from 1.8 to 2.4 cm in diameter. Local names, T., *Hayopag, Alayàn*, ex Blanco; *Cacaná* ex Vidal; *Basacan, Catabang;* Bogobo, *Ulaian;* Moro, *Ulan.*

12. **Quercus philippinensis** A. DC. Prodr. 16 ^{2} (1864) 97; F.-Vill. Nov. App. (1883) 208; Vidal Phan. Cuming. Philip. (1886) 147; Rev. Pl. Vasc. Filip. (1886) 265; Ceron Cat. Pl. Herb. (1892) 165; Wenzig in Jahrb. Bot. Gart. Berlin 4 (1886) 231.

LUZON, Province of Tayabas, Mount Banajao, *Cuming 809*, type; *Elmer 8185*, May, 1907; *For. Bur. 7910, 7911 Curran & Merritt*, November, 1907; Mount Malaraya, *For. Bur. 7848 Curran & Merritt*, November, 1907: Province of Zambales, Mount Tapulao, *For. Bur. 8100 Curran & Merritt*, December, 1907.

This species is manifestly allied to *Quercus soleriana* Vidal, but is well characterized by its very prominently caudate-acuminate leaves. It appears to be rather local. King states that he can see no reason why this species should not be reduced to *Quercus lineata* Blume, of the section *Cyclobalanopsis*, but its leaves are entire, and recently collected material from the type locality shows it to have erect male spikes, and therefore to be a true *Cyclobalanus*. Wenzig l. c. states under *Q. philippinensis:* "*Q. llanosii* DC. N. 235, *Q. ovalis* Blanco fl. de filip. (ed. 2) p. 502, DC. N. 236, *Q. Blancoi* A. DC. N. 237 * * * sunt nonnisi formae *Q. philippinensis* DC.," but *Q. llanosii* is a species very distinct from *Q. philippinensis*, while *Q. blancoi* is an exact synonym of *Q. ovalis*, which is a species entirely different from both *Q. llanosii* and *Q. philippinensis*, as shown above.

13. **Quercus bennettii** Miq. Fl. Ind. Bat. 1 ^{1} (1856) 857; DC. Prodr. 16 ^{2} (1864) 94; King in Ann. Bot. Gard. Calcutta 2 (1889) 64, *pl. 58A;* Merr. in Philip. Journ. Sci. 1 (1906) Suppl. 41.

Q. llanosii F.-Vill. Nov. App. (1883) 208; Vidal Sinopsis Atlas (1883) XLI, *t. 92, f. F.* ?, non A. DC.

Quercus wenzigiana Merr. in Philip. Journ. Sci. 1 (1906) Suppl. 41, non King.

LUZON, Province of Bataan, Lamao River, Mount Mariveles, *Williams 705*, March, 1904; *Whitford 295, 365*, May, June, 1904; *For. Bur. 54 Barnes*, October, 1903; *For. Bur. 632, 685, 759, 781 Borden*, April, May, 1904; *For. Bur. 7224 Curran*, June, 1907; *Bur. Sci. 1572 Foxworthy*, October, 1906; *Leiberg 6052*, July, 1904: Province of Zambales, Masinloc, *Merrill 2941*, May, 1903: Province of Rizal, Antipolo, *Merrill 1709*, March, 1903: Province of Tayabas, *For. Bur. 1826 Klemme*, September, 1904.

Some of the specimens from the Province of Bataan were identified by Von Seemen as *Quercus bennettii* Miq., and others as *Q. wenzigiana* King, but they are manifestly all one species, and appear to me to be closer to *Q. bennettii* Miq., than to *Q. wenzigiana*. They are certainly very close to Maingay's Malacca specimen in Herb. Kew, referred by King to Miquel's species. Local names, T., *Bayucan, Basacan, Catibang, Palonapoy.*

Malacca, Borneo, and Bangka.

14. Quercus merrillii Seem. in Fedde Repert. 5 (1908) 21.

PALAWAN, Mount Pulgar, *For. Bur. 3857, 3858 Curran*, February, March, 1906; *Bur. Sci. 566 Foxworthy*, March, 1906.

A very distinct species, known only from Mount Pulgar.

§ CHLAMYDOBALANUS.

15. Quercus cooperta Blanco Fl. Filip. ed. 2 (1845) 503.

Castanopsis costata F.-Vill. Nov. App. (1883) 209, non A. DC.

Castanea cooperta Oerst. Vidensk. Selsk. Skr. V **9** (1873) 379.

Quercus fernandezii Vidal Sinopsis Atlas (1883) XLI, *t. 92, f. E.;* Rev. Pl. Vasc. Filip. (1886) 260.

The only specimen of this species that I have seen is *Vidal 617*, from Angat, Province of Bulacan, Luzon, in Herb. Kew, a topotype of Blanco's species. Although Blanco's description is very short, I can see no particular reason for displacing his specific name, which is here accepted. Vidal placed the species in the section *Lithocarpus*, but it appears properly to belong in the section *Chlamydobalanus*.

16. Quercus reflexa King in Ann. Bot. Gard. Calcutta 2 (1889) 78, *t. 72*.

MINDANAO, District of Davao, Todaya, *Copeland 1289*, April, 1904.

This very characteristic specimen agrees closely with King's description and figure of *Quercus reflexa*. It is well distinguished by its acorns being entirely inclosed by the cups, the latter being covered with short reflexed tubercles.

Borneo.

§ LITHOCARPUS.

17. Quercus curranii sp. nov.

Arbor circiter 20 m alta, ramulis densissime ferrugineo-tomentosis; foliis oblongis vel oblongo-ellipticis, subcoriaceis, 10 ad 12 cm longis, basi acutis, apice breviter obscureque acuminatis, integris, supra nitidis, subtus pallidioribus, plus minus ferrugineo- vel cinereo-pubescentibus; cupulis turbinatis, ferrugineo-pubescentibus, supra tuberculatis, vix zonulatis, 3 cm longis crassisque.

A tree about 20 m high. Branches terete, brownish, slightly pubescent, the branchlets very densely ferruginous-tomentose. Leaves oblong or oblong-lanceolate, subcoriaceous, entire, 10 to 12 cm long, 3 to 5 cm wide, the base acute, the apex shortly and obscurely acuminate, the upper surface brownish, shining, in age glabrous, when young somewhat pubescent, especially along the midrib, the lower surface pale, somewhat cinereous-pubescent, the midrib and lateral nerves ferruginous-pubescent; nerves 9 to 11 on each side of the midrib, prominent beneath, the reticulations obscure; petioles ferruginous-tomentose, about 1 cm long. Flowers unknown. Involucre turbinate, 3 cm high and 3 cm in diameter, narrowed from the upper third to the base, and with a stout 1 cm long stalk, rather densely ferruginous-pubescent, the lower two-thirds smooth, or with very few scattered spines above, the portion covering the top of the glans with numerous stout tubercles, which become more numerous and more densely disposed towards the apex, the upper third extending over the top of the glans and nearly inclosing it, leaving a circular ostiole 1 cm in diameter or less. Glans very hard, bony, the base and sides continuous, hemispherical, the top slightly convex, the apex depressed and apiculate, about 2 cm high and nearly 3 cm in diameter.

LUZON, Province of Laguna, Mount Banajao, *For. Bur. 7917, 7918 Curran & Merritt*, November, 1907, in forests at an altitude of from 800 to 900 m.

A very characteristic species, and the only one of the section known from the Philippines, allied to *Quercus rotundata* Bl., of Java, and to *Q. pulchra* King, of Borneo, but very distinct from both. It is the species of which Vidal figured the fruits as *Quercus* sp., Sinopsis Atlas (1883) XLI, *t. 92, f. G.*, and which also came Mount Banajao, at an altitude of about 1000 m.

DOUBTFUL AND EXCLUDED SPECIES.

QUERCUS CERRIS Blanco Fl. Filip. (1837) 727; ed. 2 (1845) 503, non Linn.

It is quite impossible to determine what species Blanco had in mind, from his very short and imperfect description. It is possible that it is the same as *Quercus llanosii* A. DC.; it is, of course, not at all the European species.

The following note from Blanco's discussion of this imperfectly described species, throws much light on his methods of botanizing: "It is truly lamentable that for the lovers of the study of nature, neither prayers, supplications nor money suffice to bring to knowledge the precious things of the Philippine forests."

QUERCUS NITIDA Von Seem. in Perk. Frag. Fl. Philip. (1904) 42, non Blume.

The specimen, *Merrill 1115*, at least the one before me, is a mixture, the fruits, picked up from the ground, being very similar to those of *Q. reflexa* King, but the leaves are manifestly those of *Parinarium* (*Rosaceæ*) well characterized by the glands at the base of the lamina. *Quercus nitida* Blume is a doubtful species, and the above specimen, so far as it is a *Quercus*, does not seem to be at all allied to it.

QUERCUS CASTELLARNAUIANA Merr. in For. Bur. Bull. 1 (1903) 16; Von Seem. in Perk. Frag. Fl. Philip. (1904) 41, non Vidal.

This is an undeterminable form, as noted by Von Seemen, with flowers only. It is not Vidal's species.

The only clue we have to the numerous species credited to the Philippines in the Novissima Appendix by F.-Villar, is Vidal's notes.[15] Those accounted for by Vidal have been treated above according to the disposition Vidal made of them. It seems probable that of the nineteen species admitted by F.-Villar, none of those originally described from extra-Philippine material were correctly identified. Eight species were unaccounted for by Vidal, and it does not seem to be worth while to enter into any further consideration of them, as there are no specimens extant, and their identification would be only a matter of guesswork.

[15] Rev. Pl. Vasc. Filip. (1886) 260–265.

THE GENUS RADERMACHERA HASSK IN THE PHILIPPINES.

By ELMER D. MERRILL.

(*From the Botanical Section of the Biological Laboratory, Bureau of Science, Manila, P. I.*)

The Philippine history of this genus begins with the publication of Blanco's "Flora de Filipinas" in 1837, in which two species are inadequately described, *Millingtonia pinnata* Blanco and *Millingtonia quadripinnata* Blanco. The descriptions of both are imperfect, and both species have been variously interpreted by later authors. The descriptions are repeated in the second and third editions of Blanco's work, without change of name. In 1861, Bureau described *Radermachera banaibana* in Adansonia 2:194, based on a specimen in the Paris herbarium collected at Calauan, Province of Laguna, Luzon, by Callery. This species is manifestly the same as the one described by Blanco as *Millingtonia pinnata* and was so considered by Seemann in his Revision of the Natural Order Bignoniaceae,[1] where Blanco's *Millingtonia pinnata* is transferred to *Radermachera* as *R. pinnata* (Blanco) Seem., Bureau's *Radermachera banaibana* being reduced as a synonym. At the same time Seemann also transferred Blanco's *Millingtonia quadripinnata* to *Radermachera*, as *R. quadripinna*, and referred to it a specimen collected in the Philippines by Cuming (no. 996). In 1883, F.-Villar[2] transferred Blanco's two species of *Millingtonia* to *Stereospermum*, as *S. pinnatum* and *S. quadripinnatum*, while Naves figured a plant that he identified with *Millingtonia quadripinnata* Blanco in the third edition of Blanco's Flora de Filipinas, *t. 252*. In this same year Vidal[3] also figured a plant that he identified as *Stereospermum quadripinnatum* F.-Vill., which although poorly and imperfectly drawn, is, I am confident, identical with the plant determined by F.-Villar as *Stereospermum quadripinnatum*, and which, whether or not it is Blanco's *Millingtonia quadripinnata*, is certainly the plant he described as *M. pinnata*.

In 1884, Rolfe[4] considered the Philippine species of *Stereospermum*,

[1] Journ. Bot. **8** (1870) 147.
[2] Nov. App. 151.
[3] Sinopsis Atlas *t. 73, f. A*.
[4] Journ. Linn. Soc. Bot. **21** (1884) 313–315.

recognizing four species, *S. quadripinnatum* (Blanco) F.-Vill., the form so identified by F.-Villar and Vidal, *S. pinnatum* (Blanco) F.-Vill., to which is referred a specimen collected by Cuming (no. 1517), which is certainly not the same as the plant Blanco described, *S. banaibanai* (Bureau) Rolfe, and *S. seemannii* Rolfe, the latter described as new, based on *Cuming 996,* a very fragmentary specimen, which had been referred by Seemann to *Radermachera quadripinna*. Vidal [5] follows Rolfe in his consideration of the Philippine species of the genus. In 1905, the present author described *Radermachera elmeri,* and in the following year, *R. biternata,* this being a history of the Philippine forms up to the present time.

The difficulty has been to determine just what the plants were that Blanco described, and from an examination of his descriptions, both of which are imperfect, the conclusion has been reached that both of Blanco's descriptions apply to only one species, for which the earlier name *pinnata* is here adopted, although none of the specimens so identified have pinnate leaves, and no specimens seen from the Philippines have 4-pinnate leaves. The local name, *Banaibanai,* is almost invariably applied to the form below considered to represent *Radermachera pinnata* (Blanco) Seem., and is one of the names cited by Blanco. The other native name cited by Blanco, *Botong manoc,* meaning "chicken bone," is of little value in establishing the identity of the species, as it is applied indiscriminately by the natives to a number of totally different trees. The only native name cited by Blanco under *Millingtonia quadripinnata,* is *Baticulin,* but this name is almost invariably applied to various arborescent *Lauraceae* at the present time.

Nine species of *Radermachera* are recognized in the following paper, considerably more than is known from all other regions combined. In my treatment of the older species, based on Blanco's two Millingtonias, I am at considerable variance with Seemann, and entirely at variance with Rolfe, in my conception as to what Blanco really intended to describe, but my conclusions have been based on considerable field knowledge, extending over a period of six years, as well as a very extensive series of specimens from all parts of the Philippines, and especially rich in individual collections from the provinces about Manila, from which Blanco received most of the material on which his Flora de Filipinas was based.

[5] Phan. Cuming. Philip. (1885) 132; Rev. Pl. Vasc. Filip. (1886) 203.

KEY TO THE SPECIES.

Calyx strongly longitudinally ribbed; leaves pinnate.................... 1. *R. coriacea*
Calyx smooth, not ribbed; leaves various.
    Leaves simply pinnate .... 2. *R. elliptica*
    Leaves bi-ternate .... 3. *R. biternata*
    Leaves bi- or tripinnate.
        Corolla 4 to 6.5 cm long.
            Corolla campanulate, usually broadly so.
                Flowers about 6 cm long... 4. *R. elmeri*
                Flowers 4 to 4.5 cm long.
                      Leaflets obtuse, or shortly and obtusely acuminate............. 5. *R. fenicis*
                      Leaflets slenderly long-acuminate .... 6. *R. acuminata*
            Corolla tubular, 5.5 cm long, the limb spreading................. 7. *R. palawanensis*
        Corolla 3 cm long or less.
            Rachises of the panicles and leaves not lenticellate; flowers 2.5 to 3 cm long.
                Panicles pubescent .... 8. *R. pinnata*
                Panicles glabrous .... 8. *R. pinnata glabra*
            Rachises of the panicles and leaves usually strongly lenticellate; corolla
                less than 2 cm long.. 9. *R. mindorensis*

1. Radermachera coriacea sp. nov.

Arbor glabra; foliis pinnatis, 20 ad 30 cm longis; foliolis 5, coriaceis, supra nitidis, oblongis vel elliptico-oblongis, 7 ad 14 cm longis, basi acutis, apice obtusis vel obscure obtuseque acuminatis, marginibus recurvatis; floribus 4 cm longis; calycibus 1.8 cm longis, fissis, valde longitudinaliter costatis, angustatis; fructibus 16 cm longis.

A tree, glabrous throughout. Branches terete, brown, densely lenticellate. Leaves pinnate, 20 to 30 cm long: leaflets 5, oblong or elliptical-oblong, 7 to 14 cm long, 3 to 4 cm wide, firmly coriaceous, the upper surface very shiny, the lower slightly paler and somewhat shining, densely punctate-glandular, the base acute, the apex obtuse or shortly and obscurely blunt-acuminate, the margins rather strongly recurved; nerves about 13 on each side of the midrib, anastomosing, slightly more distinct than are the rather lax reticulations; petiolules of the lateral leaflets about 1 cm long, that of the terminal leaflet 2.5 cm long. Panicles at least 15 cm long. Calyx 1.8 cm long, narrow, strongly longitudinally costate with 5 or 6 ridges, cleft down one side nearly to the middle, 3-toothed at the apex. Corolla 4 cm long, the tube rather narrow, slightly enlarged above, the lobes about 1 cm long, obtuse. Fruit 16 cm long, the valves 5 to 7 mm wide, shining, coriaceous, glabrous, blunt or acuminate at the apex; seeds unknown.

LUZON, Province of Tayabas (Principe), Baler, *Merrill 1099*, September, 1902, N. v., *Bibit parang*.

A very characteristic species, not only in its simply pinnate leaves and very coriaceous leaflets, but also in its cleft and strongly ridged calyx. It is the only known Philippine species possessing the latter character.

2. Radermachera elliptica sp. nov.

Arbor glabra; foliis pinnatis, circiter 35 cm longis; foliolis 5, ellipticis vel obovato-ellipticis, usque ad 15 cm longis, basi acutis vel acuminatis, apice late rotundatis vel breviter obtuseque acuminatis, nervis utrinque 9; paniculis axillaribus, circiter 15 cm longis, densis; floribus 5 cm longis, calycibus 2 cm longis, obliquis, junioribus clausis; fructibus 20 ad 25 cm longis.

A tree, glabrous throughout. Branches terete, brown, strongly lenticellate. Leaves simply pinnate, about 35 cm long: leaflets 5, elliptical or obovate-elliptical, 12 to 15 cm long, 7 to 9 cm wide, coriaceous, shining, the base acute or somewhat acuminate, the apex broad, rounded, or very shortly and broadly obtusely acuminate; nerves about 9 on each side of the midrib, distinct, anastomosing, the reticulations lax; petiolules about 1.5 cm long, that of the terminal leaflet short, but the rachis produced about 5 cm beyond the upper pair of leaflets. Panicles axillary, about 15 cm long, peduncled, densely flowered, more or less resinous and shining. Flowers white. Calyx about 2 cm long, closed in bud, obliquely split in anthesis, not toothed, submembranaceous, smooth, not at all ridged. Corolla 5 cm long, the tube somewhat abruptly enlarged where it emerges from the calyx, about 1.5 cm in diameter above, the lobes broadly ovate, rounded, 1 cm long, somewhat hairy inside at the insertion of the anthers; filaments glabrous. Capsules 20 to 25 cm long, nearly cylindrical, slightly compressed, glabrous, shining, 7 to 8 mm in diameter, the apex somewhat acuminate; seeds numerous, including the wings 1.3 cm long.

LUZON, Province of Bulacan, Angat, *For. Bur. 11141 Aguilar*, April, 1908.

Well characterized by its pinnate leaves, elliptical coriaceous leaflets, and large flowers. Not closely allied to any other known Philippine species.

3. Radermachera biternata Merr. in Philip. Journ. Sci. 1 (1906) Suppl. 238.

CULION, *Merrill 568*, December, 1902. BUSUANGA, *For. Bur. 3491 Curran*, December, 1905.

The only known species of the genus with biternate leaves.

4. Radermachera elmeri Merr. in Govt. Lab. Publ. (Philip.) 29 (1905) 48.

LUZON, Province of Benguet, Sablan, *Elmer 6179* (type), April, 1904: Province of Cagayan, *Bolster 134*, July 15, 1905. PALAWAN, Balsajan River, *Bur. Sci. 584 Foxworthy*, March, 1906; Cabudlungan, *For. Bur. 5190 Curran*, August, 1906. N. v., *Agtap*, in Palawan.

This species is well characterized by its very large flowers, those in the type being 6 cm long, and, according to the collector, pink in color, while those of Bolster's specimen are 6.5 cm long and said by him to be white and more or less yellow inside. The Palawan specimens differ from the type in having somewhat smaller flowers (5.5 cm), which are said by Foxworthy to be white and fragrant. I can not, however, find any valid characters in the material at hand to warrant the separation of any of the above as distinct species, although additional material may show such a course to be desirable.

5. Radermachera fenicis sp. nov.

Arbor parva, usque ad 5 m alta, glaberrima; foliis 15 ad 20 cm longis, bipinnatis, 3-jugatis; foliolis oblongo-ellipticis vel anguste obovato-ellipticis, 4 ad 5 cm longis, subtus minutissime punctatis, apice acutis, obtusis, vel breviter obtuseque acuminatis, basi cuneatis; paniculis terminalibus folia aequantibus, angustis; floribus albis, 4 cm longis; fructibus circiter 11 cm longis.

A small tree 3 to 5 m high, glabrous throughout. Branches terete, grayish-brown, lenticellate. Leaves opposite, about 20 cm long, the lowest pinnæ 3-foliolate, the others of single leaflets: leaflets oblong-elliptical to obovate-elliptical, 4 to 5 cm long, 1.5 to 3 cm wide, rather thin, shining, the apex obtuse, acute, or somewhat acuminate, the base cuneate, the lower surface minutely punctate; lateral primary nerves about 7 on each side of the midrib, anastomosing, scarcely more distinct than are the secondary nerves and reticulations; petiolules 5 mm long or less, that of the terminal leaflet 1 to 1.5 cm long. Panicles terminal, narrow, about as long as the leaves, the bracteoles linear-setaceous, about 4 mm long. Flowers white. Calyx somewhat campanulate, epunctate, 1 cm long, 2-lobed, one lobe with two, the other with three small teeth. Corolla about 4 cm long, the first 5 mm slender, tubular, then abruptly enlarged and campanulate, 3 cm wide above, the lobes broad, rounded. Stamens glabrous. Capsules somewhat compressed, about 11 cm long, 6 mm thick, glabrous; seeds many, 3 mm wide, and, including the wings, 1 cm long, apiculate.

BATAN (Batanes Islands), Santo Domingo de Basco, *Bur. Sci. 3583 Fenix*, May, 1907. N. v., *Balaybayan*.

A species well characterized by its small leaves, comparatively short capsules, and its blunt, acute, or only shortly acuminate leaflets. I am disposed to refer here an imperfect specimen from Mindoro, *For. Bur. 9750 Merritt*, but when more and better material is secured, the Mindoro plant may be found to present characters sufficient to warrant its description as a distinct species. It has much more acuminate leaves than has the Batan plant.

6. Radermachera acuminata sp. nov.

Stereospermum quadripinnatum Rolfe in Journ. Linn. Soc. Bot. 21 (1884) 313; nec *Millingtonia quadripinnata* Blanco, nec *Radermachera quadripinna* Seem.

Arbor glabra; foliis bipinnatis, circiter 40 cm longis: foliolis oblongo-lanceolatis vel lanceolatis, coriaceis, basi acutis, apice valde acuminatis, usque ad 13 cm longis; paniculis terminalibus circiter 25 cm longis; floribus circiter 4 cm longis, campanulatis.

A tree, glabrous throughout, or the inflorescence obscurely puberulent. Leaves bipinnate, about 40 cm long, the lowermost pinnæ with 5 leaflets, the next with 3 leaflets, and the upper ones simple: leaflets oblong-lanceolate or lanceolate, 8 to 13 cm long, 2.5 to 4.5 cm wide, the base acute, the apex slenderly long-acuminate, coriaceous, slightly shining; lateral nerves about 12 on each side of the midrib, not prominent, anastomosing, the reticulations fine, indistinct; petiolules 8 to 12 mm long, that of the terminal leaflet 2.5 cm long. Panicles terminal, about 25 cm long, the primary branches about 5 cm long, many-flowered. Flowers crowded at the ends of the panicle-branches. Calyx closed in bud, in anthesis campanulate, about 1 cm long, 2-lobed. Corolla 4 cm long, the portion within the calyx slender, tubular, then abruptly enlarged and campanulate, about 2 cm wide, the lobes rounded, broad. Capsules unknown.

GUIMARAS, *For. Bur. 277 Gammill*, January, 1904.

I do not hesitate to refer here *Cuming 1003*, which Rolfe considered to represent Blanco's *Millingtonia quadripinnata*, but which is certainly not Blanco's species. I am disposed to refer here also an immature specimen from Masbate, *Whitford 1696*, and also a very fragmentary specimen from Mount Abu, Pampanga Province, Luzon, *Foxworthy 1949*. The exact locality of Cuming's specimen cited above is unknown, Rolfe stating it as Province of Albay, Luzon, but Cuming's list at Kew giving this number as from the Province of Pangasinan.

7. Radermachera palawanensis sp. nov.

Arbuscula subglabra; ramulis, rhachidibus, paniculisque sparse pubescentibus; foliis circiter 20 cm longis, bipinnatis; foliolis oblongo-ellipticis vel lanceolato-ellipticis, coriaceis, nitidis, 3.5 ad 8 cm longis, basi acutis, apice acuminatis, margine revolutis; paniculis folia aequantibus, laxis, paucifloris; floribus albis, 5 ad 5.5 cm longis; corollae tubo cylindraceo.

A shrub, nearly glabrous, or the branches, rachises of the leaves, and panicles slightly pubescent. Leaves about 20 cm long, bipinnate, the lowest pair of pinnæ with 5 leaflets, the next with 3 leaflets, the upper ones simple: leaflets oblong-elliptical or lanceolate-elliptical, 3.5 to 8 cm long, 1 to 2.5 cm wide, coriaceous, glabrous, shining on both surfaces, the margins rather strongly recurved, the base acute, the apex more or less acuminate, sometimes apiculate, and rarely with one or two irregular teeth at the apex; lateral nerves about 8 on each side of the midrib, not very distinct, anastomosing; petiolules of the lateral leaflets 3 to 8 mm long, that of the terminal one longer. Panicles as long as the leaves, lax, few-flowered. Flowers white. Calyx subcylindrical, narrowed below, obscurely lobed, about 1 cm long. Corolla 5 to 5.5 cm long, the portion within the calyx very slender, tubular, then abruptly enlarged, forming a broader tubular portion 2 to 2.5 cm long, the limb spreading, about 3 cm in diameter, the lobes broad, rounded. Capsules very slender, about 20 cm long, the valves at least 3 mm wide; seeds unknown.

PALAWAN, Victoria Peak, *Bur. Sci. 699 Foxworthy*, March 23, 1906, on rocky slopes along a river at 1,000 m altitude.

8. Radermachera pinnata (Blanco) Seem. in Journ. Bot. 8 (1870) 147.

Millingtonia pinnata Blanco Fl. Filip. (1837) 501; ed. 2 (1845) 351; ed. 3, 2: 285; Miq. Fl. Ind. Bat. 2 (1856) 753.

Millingtonia quadripinnata Blanco l. cc. 499, 351, 286; Miq. l. c.

Radermachera banaibana Bur. in Adansonia 2 (1861) 194; Seem. in Journ. Bot. 8 (1870) 147; Merr. in Philip. Journ. Sci. 1 (1906) Suppl. 124.

Stereospermum banaibanai Rolfe in Journ. Linn. Soc. Bot. 21 (1884) 314; Vidal Rev. Pl. Vasc. Filip. (1886) 203; Phan. Cuming. Philip. (1885) 132.

Stereospermum seemannii Rolfe in Journ. Linn. Soc. Bot. 21 (1884) 314; Vidal l. cc. 132, 203.

Stereospermum quadripinnatum F.-Vill. Nov. App. (1883) 151; Vidal Sinopsis Atlas (1883) *t. 73, f. A* (inaccurate).

Radermachera quadripinna Seem. in Journ. Bot. 8 (1870) 147.

Stereospermum pinnatum F.-Vill. Nov. App. (1883) 151.

LUZON, without locality, *Cuming 1182, 996:* Province of Benguet, Sablan, *Elmer 6157,* April, 1904: Province of Zambales, *For. Bur. 5800 Curran,* January, 1907; *For. Bur. 6084 Aguilar,* January, 1907; Botolan, *Merrill 2925:* Province of Pangasinan, Salasa, *For. Bur. 9628 Zschokke,* December, 1907: Province of Rizal, Montalban, *Loher 4323,* March, 1891; Antipolo, *Merrill 1729,* March, 1903: Province of Bataan, Mount Mariveles, *Whitford 24,* April, 1904; *For. Bur. 725, 1540, 1541, 1550, 1542, 1566 Borden; For. Bur. 342, 185, 548 Barnes; For. Bur. 2424 Meyer,* January, 1905; *Williams 588,* February, 1904: Province of Camarines Sur, *Ahern 61,* February, 1902. MINDORO, *For. Bur. 9717 Merritt,* February, 1908.

Var. **glabra** var. nov.

Differt a typo omnibus partibus glabratis.

LUZON, Province of Rizal, Bosoboso, *For. Bur. 2671 Ahern's collector,* January, 1905 (type); Antipolo, *For. Bur. 469 Ahern's collector; Dec. Philip. For. Fl. 174; Loher 4322,* March, 1903: Province of Bataan, Mount Mariveles, *For. Bur. 2469 Borden,* January, 1905; *Bur. Sci. 5177 Foxworthy,* April, 1908: Province of Cagayan, *For. Bur. 6660, 11303 Klemme,* April, 1907, 1908: Province of Isabela, Casiguran, *Bur. Sci. 3121 Mearns,* June, 1907. MINDANAO, Lake Lanao, Camp Keithley, *Mrs. Clemens 274,* February, 1906.

This is the most common and widely distributed species of the genus in the Philippines, being somewhat variable, and its synonomy is rather complicated, due primarily to Blanco's imperfect descriptions, and to various later interpretations of these. The leaves are bi- and tripinnate, frequently on the same specimen, and the flowers vary in size from 2.5 to 3 cm in length, but on all the specimens cited above, both under the species and the variety, the flowers are uniformly described by the collectors, as far as the field notes show, as pink or pale purple and marked with yellow inside.

I have adopted the first valid specific name available, taken from *Millingtonia pinnata* Blanco, although so far as I have observed, and in the large series of specimens examined, the leaves are never simply pinnate. It is universally known to the natives as *Banaibanai,* a name normally applied to no other species, other than the following one, and with the exception of the discrepancy as to leaves, Blanco's description applies very closely. The species is very abundant in the regions from which Blanco received most of his material. The disposition of Blanco's *Millingtonia quadripinnata* necessitated careful consideration, but I have here reduced it to *Radermachera pinnata* (Blanco) Seem., although in this I am at variance with both Seemann and Rolfe, who have previously worked over the Philippine species of this genus. Knowing thoroughly the flora of the region about Manila, and the contiguous provinces, it does not seem probable that this species, if distinct from *R. pinnata,* as considered by Blanco, should have escaped our notice, but up to the present time there is nothing in our herbarium to which Blanco's description applies so well as to the material here considered to represent *Radermachera pinnata.* It seems rather curious that Blanco should have described it under two different names, neither of which apply well to the species, for none of the above specimens have simply pinnate leaves, and none have quadripinnate ones, all having bi- or tripinnate leaves or both. Blanco's work shows internal evidence that the various species were described from time to time, in a period extending over many years, sometimes from fresh material, at other times from dried specimens brought or sent to him by various persons. It seems very evident, moreover, that he had no herbarium, so that the probability of repetitions was thereby increased.

As to *Stereospermum seemannii* Rolfe, after an examination of several specimens of each of the numbers secured by Cuming, including the type of *S. seemannii*, I can see no reason for separating it from *Radermachera pinnata*. The type, *Cuming 996*, and such duplicates of the type number as I have seen, one of which is before me, are very fragmentary, with detached leaflets and badly insect-eaten flowers, and appear to be in all respects the same as Blanco's species.

9. Radermachera mindorensis sp. nov.

Stereospermum pinnatum Rolfe in Journ. Linn. Soc. Bot. 21 (1884) 314; Vidal Rev. Pl. Vasc. Filip. (1886) 203, not *Millingtonia pinnata* Blanco.

Stereospermum quadripinnatum Naves in Fl. Filip. ed. 3, t. 252?

Arbor glabra, usque ad 20 m alta; foliis tripinnatis, rariter bipinnatis, 40 ad 50 cm longis; foliolis lanceolatis vel oblongo-lanceolatis, basi acutis, apice caudato-acuminatis, chartaceis, 8 ad 11 cm longis; paniculis terminalibus, diffusis, folia aequantibus vel longioribus; floribus circiter 1.5 cm longis.

A tree glabrous throughout, about 20 m high. Branches terete, brown or gray, lenticellate. Leaves tripinnate, rarely bipinnate, 40 to 50 cm long, the rachis lenticellate; leaflets lanceolate or oblong-lanceolate, chartaceous, somewhat shining, 8 to 11 cm long, 2 to 3.5 cm wide, the base acute or somewhat acuminate, the apex slenderly caudate-acuminate, the acumen about 2 cm long, acute; nerves about 12 on each side of the midrib, anastomosing, slightly more distinct than are the secondary ones and reticulations; petiolules of the lateral leaflets about 5 mm long, those of the terminal leaflets 1 to 2 cm long. Panicles terminal, glabrous, diffuse, equaling or longer than the leaves, the rachis frequently lenticellate. Flowers light-purple. Calyx somewhat campanulate, 4 to 5 mm long, closed in bud, in anthesis shortly and irregularly 3- to 5-toothed. Corolla 1.5 to 1.8 cm long, the portion within the calyx slender, tubular, then abruptly enlarged and tubular-campanulate, somewhat pubescent on the outside, irregularly lobed. Capsules 45 cm long, 4 to 5 mm in diameter, somewhat compressed; seeds, including the wings, about 13 mm long.

MINDORO, Calapan, *Merrill 893* (type), April, 1903; Pola, *Merrill 2240, 2473*, May, June, 1903; Bongabong River, *Whitford 1387*, January, 1906; Baco River, *McGregor 257*, April, 1905, with larger flowers than the type; Bongabong, *Hickman s. n.*

Allied to the preceding species, but with much more diffuse panicles, and much smaller flowers. I am disposed to refer here *Cuming 1517*, which was from the Island of Mindoro, according to Cuming's list at Kew, not from Batangas Province, Luzon, according to the labels on some of the specimens. It was referred by Rolfe to *Stereospermum pinnatum* F.-Vill., but the sheet at Kew, which I have examined, has at least bipinnate leaves, and not pinnate ones as stated by Rolfe, and is certainly not the same as *Millingtonia pinnata* Blanco.

Printed by Libri Plureos GmbH in Hamburg,
Germany